Assessment in Action in the Primary School

Primary Directions Series

Series Editors: Colin Conner, School of Education, University of Cambridge UK and Geoff Southworth, Department of Education Studies and Management, University of Reading

Assessment in Action in the Primary School
Edited by Colin Conner

Assessment in Action in the Primary School

Edited by

Colin Conner

UK	Falmer Press, 1 Gunpowder Square, London, EC4A 3DE
USA	Falmer Press, Taylor & Francis Inc., 325 Chestnut Street, 8th Floor, Philadelphia, PA 19106

First published in 1999

A catalogue record for this book is available from the British Library

ISBN 0 7507 0953 7 cased
ISBN 0 7507 0952 9 paper

Library of Congress Cataloging-in-Publication Data are available on request

Jacket design by Caroline Archer

Typeset in 10/12pt Garamond by
Graphicraft Limited, Hong Kong

Printed in Great Britain by Biddles Ltd., Guildford and King's Lynn on paper which has a specified pH value on final paper manufacture of not less than 7.5 and is therefore 'acid free'.

Contents

List of Figures

List of Contributors

Colin Conner is a lecturer in primary education at the University of Cambridge School of Education.

Mary-Jane Drummond is a lecturer in primary education at the University of Cambridge School of Education.

Peter Dudley is a senior adviser (school development) in the Essex Learning Services Directorate.

Ros Frost teaches in a primary school in Essex.

Philip Hewett is the headteacher of the Leys Primary School in Hertfordshire.

Sue Swaffield is Senior Adviser (curriculum and assessment) in Cambridgeshire.

Sally Threllfall is quality assurance officer within the Integrated Early Years Development Team of Leeds City Council.

Jenny Woodbridge is a primary adviser for early years, City of York Education Department.

Acknowledgments

As editor of this publication, I would like to thank the contributors for a series of thought-provoking reflections on assessment issues currently facing primary schools. I am also grateful to: Laurence Pollinger Limited and the Estate of Frieda Lawrence Ravagli for permission to include an extract from D.H. Lawrence's poem 'Work'; to Bensley and Kilby for the inclusion of Figure 2.1, an extract from their baseline assessment materials; to Andrew Pollard for Figure 2.4, which comes from page 241 of his publication *The Social World of Children's Learning*; to HMSO for permission to include Figure 3.2; to Leeds City Council Department of Education for the inclusion of materials from their *Framework for Entry Assessment*; to Professor Michael Barber for permission to include his self-esteem/expectations matrix as Figure 7.4, and to Essex LEA for permission to include examples from their Learning Perception Survey materials, *What I Think about School*.

Series Editor's Preface

This series aims to produce a set of key texts which focus upon a range of significant topics in primary education and schooling. The timing of the series is significant in that it attempts to draw together past and present understanding of primary phase issues. Taking advantage of the psychological influence of the close of a century and the beginning of a new millennium, the series aims to provide a set of books which draw together the main insights, contemporary challenges and future issues facing primary education.

Amongst these, assessment has been a topic of both interest and concern to primary practitioners. The introduction of the National Curriculum and its assessment arrangements in 1988 created considerable difficulties and challenges to many primary teachers. This publication indicates the considerable developments that have taken place since that time. Drawing upon the experience of primary teachers, primary advisers and University researchers, this book offers an insight into effective assessment in the primary school.

Geoff Southworth
Colin Conner
August 1999

Introduction

Colin Conner

Since the introduction of the National Curriculum in 1988, it is probably fair to say that the issue that has created the greatest tension for primary schools has been assessment. The continual changing of curriculum expectations and assessment requirements, and the more recent demands for the careful quantitative analysis of assessment results to inform decision making, has left many schools uncertain about exactly what is expected of them. This trend has been exacerbated by the recent requirement from the DfEE that schools will be required to set appropriate targets for school, class and individual improvement from 1998. This process is dependent on effective systems of assessment and appropriate processes of analysis being in place. This book explores the changes in assessment practice since the introduction of the National Curriculum, raises questions about assessment that are in the best interests of learners and provide illustrations of effective practice in action.

The chapters which follow will be of interest to students in training as a means of introducing them to the issues involved. Assessment coordinators in schools will also find the content of relevance, in that it provides a means of evaluating the effectiveness of practice in their schools. It will also be of value to teachers on courses of advanced study and to those following the National Professional Qualification for Headteachers, which emphasizes the importance of reflecting on assessment data for school improvement.

The main intention of the contributions has been to reflect on the development of assessment from their perspective and to consider the recent past, the present and what the future appears to indicate. Contributors represent the full range of the education spectrum, from class teacher to headteacher, from LEA inspector to university lecturer.

The opening chapter presents a review of some of the current issues associated with assessment in the primary school. It starts by reflecting on the ways in which the term assessment has been interpreted, from 'hard-nosed objectivity' where the purpose of assessment is seen as a sifting and sorting mechanism, to a more positive view of assessment where the main purpose is to help learners achieve their potential. This is followed by a consideration of the contrasting theories that underpin assessment practice and suggests that our understanding of assessment is influenced by our views of the learning process. A distinction is drawn between a psychometric conception of assessment, which is influenced by psychological theories of intelligence developed at the turn of the century, and an educational perspective, which bases interpretations on a social constructivist view of learning. Social constructivism sees learners as active constructors of their own understanding. Learning from this perspective is influenced by what the learner currently knows and the context in which both learning and assessment take place. The implications of this perspective for assessment are considered.

Other influencing factors are also discussed, in particular issues related to the credibility, reliability and validity of assessment. One particularly significant feature that has emerged in recent research concerns the feedback which teachers provide for children about their learning. Drawing on the work of Gipps, McCallum and Brown (1997) and Black and Wiliam (1998), the implications of this are considered and suggestions offered for making feedback more effective. The chapter concludes by presenting a review of current and future expectations regarding target setting and offers some salutary comments on teachers' experience to date.

Chapter 2, by Mary Jane Drummond, focuses on the assessment of the youngest children in school using baseline assessment schemes. Despite some reservation about the necessity of formalizing assessment processes for children at such an early age and stage in their school career, she presents a very strong and convincing set of arguments that if baseline is to be applied, as we now know schools are required to do, it must be based upon a clearly espoused and agreed set of principles. She presents six propositions that should help educators shape effective baseline practice. The first of these argues that baseline assessment should only be undertaken if there is clarity about the differences between purposes and the outcomes, that is, what a scheme intends against what it actually does in practice. Second, she emphasizes that baseline assessment should not be undertaken unless educational intentions are clear. Internal value systems need to be made explicit, what it is believed education can and should do for children, and the way assessment practice supports or hinders these aspirations. The third proposition suggests that it is essential for teachers to distinguish the extent to which schemes assess for convergence, the way in which pupils are alike, or divergence, the ways in which they differ. Is assessment about the whole range of competence or concerned with potential SATs results? For Drummond, a worthwhile baseline assessment system should reflect 'each child's unique characteristics' and 'each child's individual understanding of how the world works and what is important in it'. The fourth proposition emphasizes the importance of the emotions in the assessment process and asks, does baseline assessment contribute to children's 'emotional well-being', or does it reinforce low self-esteem, lack of confidence and a fear of failure? Fifth, she argues that baseline assessment schemes should recognize the distinction which exists between learning and attainment. All children learn, but not all children attain at the same rate. Focusing on attainment, the end of the process, distracts attention from learning, the on-going process. The final proposition suggests that baseline assessment schemes must be based upon a carefully worked out set of principles which underpin practice and are enacted in practice.

Chapter 3 is written by Ros Frost, a primary teacher who is in the process of completing a Masters degree. In her contribution, she presents a summary of an investigation she undertook for her course which focused on elements of the assessment practice in her school, in particular, the school's record of achievement which had been developed over a number of years. Concern about its effectiveness and the extent to which it fulfilled its intended purposes had been raised by an external assessment review undertaken by an LEA adviser. Her investigation illustrates the importance of school based enquiry for school improvement. As Walker (1985) has argued, such engagement is now seen as an essential element of the teacher's role, 'As teaching has become increasingly professionalised and the management of educational organisations more systematised, so "enquiry" has become something that teachers are expected to include in their repertoire of skills' (1985: 3). The chapter opens with an attempt to summarize her experience of assessment over the past ten years, having qualified in 1988, the year in which the Education Reform Act introduced assessment as a formal requirement in primary schools. In the early days of her teaching experience she regarded assessment as a 'beast', which placed conflicting and time consuming demands upon her. With experience and growing confidence, she began to 'tame the beast', and to reflect upon the most appropriate purposes of assessment and concluded that the primary aim of assessment should be to support children in their learning. The school's record of achievement also intended to do that, but appeared to be falling short. By interviewing colleagues and a sample of children, a range of suggestions for improvement were developed.

In Chapter 4, Philip Hewett, the headteacher of a primary school, presents an illustration of the reality of the current requirements for target setting in the primary school. He demonstrates the importance of placing target setting in the context of wider school improvement initiatives. He emphasizes that making 'significant, sound, sustainable educational progress is, in athletics terms, more like being a long distance runner than a sprinter'. He argues that success in target setting should be judged by how close a school gets to its targets rather than an expectation of always achieving or exceeding them. It is important, he suggests, for success to be judged against the previous achievement of a particular group for whom the target has been set rather than past year groups. The most difficult task is not how to set targets, but how to bring about the intended improvement. He advocates the use of 'rolling averages' for judging a school's progress and performance rather than year-on-year comparison as is currently the case with much of National Curriculum assessment. Rolling averages are produced by averaging a school's assessment results for different age groups over a period of three years rather than single year comparisons. The benefits of this process are that it removes the peaks and troughs of progress caused by the varying abilities of different cohorts of children. When the demands for setting targets and the careful analysis of assessment data were first required of schools Philip Hewett was highly sceptical, but the experience of the last three years suggests that the processes involved have resulted in significant improvements in his school. A major feature of practice at the school is that responsibility for the analysis of assessment results and the identification of implications and targets which emerge are delegated to the teachers within their respective year groups. As a result, teachers are in much greater control of the process.

Sue Swaffield is a senior adviser for curriculum and assessment in her local education authority. In Chapter 5, she presents a review of the changing nature of LEA responsibilities for assessment since the introduction of the National Curriculum and its assessment arrangements. She draws upon the continuum of LEA support developed by Riley and Rowles (1997) who distinguish between interventionist, interactive and responsive and non-interventionist LEAs, to describe the different ways in which LEAs have fulfilled their statutory assessment responsibilities. Through a case study of a primary school in her own LEA of Cambridgeshire, Swaffield illustrates the ways in which she has worked with schools. She emphasizes that in the pressure to respond to the external demands of assessment, there has been insufficient opportunity to focus upon the principles underpinning assessment practice, an emphasis on *how* rather than *why*. The chapter concludes by suggesting that LEAs will need to devote more energy in the future to reinforcing the role of assessment *for* learning rather than the current obsession with assessment *of* learning.

Consideration of the role of the LEA continues in Chapter 6, which is written by Sally Threllfall and Jenny Woodbridge, who at the time of writing both worked for the City of Leeds Education Department. The chapter provides a reflective explanation of the development and implementation of the Leeds baseline assessment system. The principles argued for by Mary Jane Drummond are central to this baseline scheme, which stresses that any assessment of children at the age of entry to school needs to be both sensitive and sensitively implemented. At the heart of the scheme are the observations that early years teachers undertake throughout their daily contact with children. These are described in Mary Jane Drummond's chapter as the '. . . rich, respectful accounts of each child's learning, past, present, and in the very near future'. Such observational descriptions of young children's learning and progress are very similar to the concept of 'documentation' developed by educators in the Emilia-Romagna region of Italy, which has a world wide reputation for the quality of its early years practice. The Leeds scheme aims to help teachers to develop their observational and judgmental skills more systematically and emphasizes the importance of the qualitative data that the process generates. In response to government demands, quantitative criteria have been developed to supplement the scheme and ensure its accreditation. As was suggested in Chapter 1, however, children's previous experience is valued by the scheme and therefore close contact with parents is essential. The data generated by this baseline scheme has been seen to promote dialogue about assessment and judgment among colleagues who have used the materials, and there are indications that it is having an effect on classroom practice. A classroom environment which allows children some responsibility for their learning, and which provides facilities and resources so that children are able to demonstrate their progress and achievements is essential. Similarly, a range of classroom tasks that capture the childrens' interests without always requiring the support of the teacher creates time for teachers to observe. The analysis of the data and the messages it offers has also emerged as important issues. In particular, the recognition that in the assessment of young children trends over time are more important than snap judgments based upon limited observation or the allocation of numerical scores. Quantitative data is not rejected, however, and its usefulness lies in its accuracy, not the volume of its figures or percentages. Initially, quantitative data is used to cause teachers to question their assessments and to combat underestimation of children's capabilities. The qualitative data produced by the use of carefully constructed observation schedules provides the detail and illustrative evidence of judgments which can then be subjected to critical scrutiny by others to confirm judgments or to cause teachers to rethink.

Chapters 7 and 8 are written by Peter Dudley, senior adviser for school development in Essex. These two chapters draw upon his work in an LEA School Improvement project. Chapter 7 focuses upon the increasing volume of assessment data that now finds its way into school and asks questions about how schools should respond to it so that it is in the best interests of learners. He argues that there is a need to clarify what the word data means to teachers and that in managing its use in school there is a need to understand the psychology of data, how people respond to it and how its analysis affects people's actions and motivations. He believes that the success of target setting as an improvement strategy is dependent on attitudes towards data and that it is essential that a positive psychology is developed. As a result, he argues that thought needs to be given to developing teachers' understanding of data as well as the skills of analysis associated with its interpretation.

Chapter 8 reinforces the importance of involving learners in the process of reflecting upon school developments. There is evidence from a range of projects that two key factors influence achievement, self-esteem and the learner's engagement with school. Dudley discusses the implementation of a pupil survey which explores these areas and discusses teachers' reactions to what pupils say about their school, their learning and their progress. He argues that the main purposes of such surveys is to promote discussion about pupil perceptions of learning and to raise questions or issues that can be investigated further by staff. It is not intended that they should provide answers.

The survey he describes has been used with children throughout the primary age range and aims to elicit responses to six areas of pupil perception which research indicates influences pupil achievement. The six areas are:

- the child's view of him or herself as a learner;
- the learners' clarity about the purposes of their learning;
- the feedback strategies that are used by teachers;
- the relationships that exist in the school and classroom and the extent to which the teacher is seen as a collaborator in the learning process;

- the pupil's perceptions of parent/home support for learning and of the collaboration between parent(s) and school;
- pupil perceptions of peer commitment to learning and their perceptions of future learning and achievement.

Careful assessment is regarded as fundamental to each of these areas and a valuable means of identifying which features prevent achievement and block progress and which support it. As he suggests, however, pupil perception data has to come with a health warning, 'Pupil perceptions can be eye opening and supportive but they can also be bruising.' He raises some important questions for those who choose to use such data gathering techniques: Are you ready for what their research data might bring? Are you going to give it the weight it deserves or are you going to deny the data that does not fit your perceptions? How will you resolve such dilemmas?'

The proliferation of assessment data and the publication of league tables of raw examination results has been dismissed by many teachers as an unfair means of comparing one school with another. This has led to increasing acceptance of 'value-added' approaches to data, which focus on pupil progress rather than the raw data of a school's assessment results. Value-added approaches compare similar schools with each other in terms of the relative progress of groups of similar pupils. In this way a school in which pupils make a lot of progress can have this recognized through the value they have added, even though the school may be a long way down a raw results league table. It is arguments of this kind that convinced the government of the need to develop bench mark tables that allow schools to compare themselves with similar schools when account is taken of the numbers of students taking free school meals and for whom English is a second language. The final chapter reviews the evidence related to value-added analyses of schools' assessment results and draws upon a small-scale research project which investigated primary schools' reactions to value-added analyses. Although it is recognized that value-added approaches to comparing schools has some strengths, there are weaknesses, and reference is made to Drummond (1993), who has argued that in assessment there is an overwhelming tendency to measure not what is of most value, but what is most easily measured. This chapter concludes by emphasizing that it is important to remember that value-added analyses focus upon a relatively small part of a school's activities and that schools have responsibility for encouraging children's learning and development across a much wider range of areas than is represented in school league tables.

Throughout the contributions to this book a number of dominant themes emerge which have implications for assessment in the future. The first relates to the principles underpinning our assessment practice. A number of writers and researchers (Conner, 1991; Drummond, 1993; James, 1998) have stressed how important it is to be clear about why we are doing something, and give justification for our practice. The assessment debate since the 1988 Education Act has been dominated by concerns about *what* is to be assessed and *how* it is to be assessed rather than clarification as to *why* something should be assessed. It is interesting that at the time of writing, the same concern has been raised about the National Curriculum itself and that the newly established Qualifications and Assessment Agency (QAA) are proposing to produce a series of statements concerning the aims of the National Curriculum and the specific purposes of the curriculum for respective age groups. Perhaps it is time that this happened for assessment at each of our stages of education.

A second theme that emerges reminds us that assessment is as much an affective issue as it is a cognitive one. How a learner feels influences how he or she performs. It is essential, therefore, that we develop ways of accessing as wide a range of information about learners in order that assessment is undertaken fairly and fully represents an individual's achievements. The knowledge of parents about their children is an important and often undervalued resource, especially in the early stages of their education. Similarly, the children themselves are an important information source, not only about their progress, but also about their learning experience and the effectiveness of the teaching and the fairness of the assessment strategies that have been employed.

A third theme draws together a range of strategies related to the improvement of assessment practice. There is evidence in a number of the chapters about the importance of dialogue. Discussion about assessment is crucially important in improving consistency, clarifying criteria and making valid and reliable judgments. Discussions about assessment cause us to question our assumptions and expectations in the best interests of learners. Reflection on assessment also stimulates an examination of the importance of context in assessment. Who assesses, how assessment is organized and managed and when and where an assessment takes place all fundamentally influence the opportunities children have to demonstrate their achievements. At a broader level, a school's context is also highly influential in the judgments that are made about a school, and the way in which such evidence is presented can effect judgments about its achievements.

Fourth, it is evident that the future of assessment is closely allied to developments in the area of school improvement. A whole range of school improvement initiatives are based upon careful analysis of assessment data. This raises a number of important implications. Most of the analysis to date tends to emphasize the importance of quantitative data, whereas arguments offered in several chapters emphasize that qualitative data is just as important, offering the detail by which numerical information can be interpreted and explained. A number of the contributions stress the importance of training in the analysis of data, however, and that at this time, much of the analysis tends to be rather naïve. Development in the skills of analysis and further experience should enable teachers, and especially headteachers, to decide which data merits detailed reflection and what can be ignored as well as the kinds of data that truly represent a child's achievements.

Finally, a number of contributions argue that the way in which learning is perceived influences assessment practice. Several of the chapters emphasize that views about the nature of learning have changed dramatically over the last 20 years. Although many educators accept the importance of the role of the learners in their own development and progress, politicians and decision makers often carry a contradictory view of learning which is derived from theories of learning developed earlier this century. As Shepard (1992) argues,

> . . . many educational policy decisions . . . are based implicitly on policy makers' own 'theories' about what conditions of education will foster student learning. If they are unaware of new research findings about how children learn, policy makers are apt to rely on their own implicit theories which probably were shaped by theories that were current when they themselves attended school. Scientific knowledge about the development of intellectual ability and learning is vastly different today than was known 40 or 50 years ago. Some things that psychologists can prove today even contradict the popular wisdom of several decades ago. Therefore, if policy makers proceed to implement outmoded theories or tests based on old theories, they might actually subvert their intended goal — of providing a rigorous and high quality education for all students. (1992: 301)

The implication which arises from this is that there is a need for politicians and policy makers to be educated to understand the justification of current views about the learning process. This is not to reject alternative perspectives but to reinforce the need to clarify when a particular view of learning is appropriate to a particular view of assessment. As has been suggested, principles should be the starting point for the deliberation about assessment, and as far as learning is concerned the focus of the future should be more concerned with *assessment for learning* rather than with *assessment of learning.*

References

BLACK, P. and WILIAM, D. (1988) *Inside the Black Box: Raising Standards Through Classroom Assessment*, London: Kings College School of Education.

CONNER, C. (1991) *Assessment and Testing in the Primary School*, London: Falmer Press.

DRUMMOND, M.J. (1993) *Assessing Children's Learning*, London: Fulton.

GIPPS, C., McCALLUM, B. and BROWN, M. (1997) 'Models of teacher assessment among primary school teachers in England', *The Curriculum Journal*, **7**, 2, pp. 167–83.

JAMES, M. (1998) *Using Assessment for School Improvement*, London: Heinemann.

RILEY, K. and ROWLES, D. (1997) 'Inspection and School Improvement in England and Wales: National contexts and local realities', Chapter 5 in TOWNSEND, T. (ed.) 1997, *Restructuring and Quality: Issues for Tomorrow's Schools*, London: Routledge.

SHEPARD, L. (1992) 'What policy makers who mandate tests should know about the new psychology of intellectual ability and learning', Concluding Commentary in GIFFORD, B.R. and O'CONNOR, M.C. (eds), *Changing Assessments: Alternative Views of Aptitude, Achievement and Instruction*, London: Kluwer Academic Publishers.

WALKER, R. (1985) *Doing Research: A Handbook for Teachers*, London: Methuen.

1   Assessment in the Primary School: A Review of Current Issues*

Colin Conner

Introduction

Assessment is an extremely topical and important issue in education at the present time and it is one that is the subject of international debate. In the United Kingdom, changes in assessment practice have affected all stages of education. James (1996), for example, suggests that from early years education through to adult education the purposes, content, form and methods of assessment are the subject of reflection, analysis and modification. James lists the following examples to illustrate the range of the current assessment debate as it currently effects all levels of the education service:

- the assessment of young children entering school, including 'baseline' assessment;
- the introduction of National Curriculum assessment and testing for school pupils from 5 to 14 in England and Wales and comparable arrangements in Scotland and Northern Ireland;
- the diagnostic assessment of children with special educational needs for the purposes of statementing and the allocation of special resource provision;
- the nature and value of examinations at 16+, especially coursework elements in the GCSE;
- the construction and use of league tables of test and examination results and the relative advantages and disadvantages of 'raw' or 'value-added' versions;
- the development of vocational assessment post 16 (NVQs and GNVQs) and the relationship with the academic 'gold standard' of A levels;
- the assessment of modular courses in further and higher education and the accreditation of prior learning (APL) and prior experiential learning (APEL);
- work-based assessment and performance appraisal.

Many of these issues are not of immediate relevance to primary teachers, but since the introduction of the 1988 Education Act it is probably true to say

---

* This is an extended version of a chapter in Whitebread, D. (1999) *The Psychology of Teaching and Learning in Primary School*, London: Routledge.

that one of the most significant effects on primary education has been the overwhelming demands of the assessment process. It has resulted in considerable additional expectations being placed upon primary teachers and has been the subject of continual change. It might have been hoped that we would move into a period of calm and a return to common sense with a change of government in 1997, but it is clear that this is not to be. The government white paper, *Excellence in Schools* emphasizes that,

> Our drive to improve children's literacy and numeracy skills will be assisted by *rigorous assessment and testing at ages 7 and 11*. In addition, SCAA supplied all primary schools earlier this year with optional tests in English and mathematics (including mental arithmetic) for 9 year olds. *We expect these to be widely used.* (DfEE, 1997: para. 2.36) [It is also expected that optional tests will be available for 8- and 10-year-olds.]

The white paper also recognizes that our education system is among the most extensively assessed in the world and clearly proposes to keep up this momentum: 'We already hold much more comprehensive data than is held in other countries. We are consulting on proposals for further improvements in the collection, dissemination and use of pupil performance and comparative data through better use of IT . . .' (para. 3.6).

But have we learned anything from our experience of the last ten years? This chapter draws upon some of the research evidence related to the implementation of national curriculum assessment and considers what it tells us about effective ways of assessing children's learning. The next section opens the debate by a reflection on some of the different ways in which assessment has been interpreted.

Contrasting views about assessment and its associated purposes

> Assessment of school children is an inexact science. We are hampered in our endeavours by both the misconceptions of history and the misrepresentations of politics. Our children are owed more than this. (Pauline Lyseight-Jones, 1994)

Whenever the word *assessment* is used, it can conjure up a wide variety of images. Rows of desks in quiet examination halls, working to a set deadline, trying to remember the answers to obscure and seemingly irrelevant questions. Sometimes it dredges up long-forgotten memories of the 11+, taking a musical examination, a driving test, an interview, or being observed in a classroom. Often, these memories are tinged with uncertainty, unhappiness, and even a feeling of failure. It is important to remember therefore, that assessment for many of us has been an emotional experience, and it is not surprising that we should reject placing learners in such situations too early in their lives. However, assessment is open to many interpretations. David Satterly (1989: 1) in his study of assessment in schools suggests that one view of assessment is as,

'. . . hard nosed objectivity, an obsession with the measurement of performances (many of which are assumed to be relatively trivial), and an increasingly technical vocabulary which defies most teachers . . .' Alternatively assessment is seen as a sifting and sorting mechanism, '. . . a means by which schools and teachers sort out children for occupations of different status in a hierarchically ordered society' (Satterly, 1989: 1).

The classic list of assessment purposes comes from Macintosh and Hale (1976), who identified six main purposes for assessment;

- **diagnosis**: finding out what precisely a student or group of students has learned with a view to planning curriculum and teaching to meet their needs;
- **evaluation**: using assessment information as evidence in judging the value of educational provision;
- **guidance**: helping students to make appropriate career or course choices;
- **grading**: identifying the level at which a student is performing and assigning a number or letter to signify the standard attained;
- **selection**: identifying those students most suitable for a particular class, school or form of employment;
- **prediction**: identifying the potential or aptitude of individuals for a particular kind of training or employment in order to avoid the waste of talent.

The influence of these ideas can be seen in the comments of more recent writers on assessment. Harlen (1994), for example has suggested that assessment in education takes place in a wide variety of contexts and for many different purposes. She suggests that those concerning individual pupils might include informing the next steps in teaching, summarizing achievement at a certain time or for the purposes of selection, certification or guidance. In this context, Harlen suggests that, 'A comprehensive definition of assessment includes the processes of gathering, interpreting, recording and use of information about a pupil's response to an educational task' (1994: 11). She adds that pupils can also be assessed for other more external purposes such as part of national surveys of educational achievement or for research purposes. This overview of potential interpretations and purposes of assessment can be extended further. For example, Berwick (1994) identified two main categories, those concerned with the educational development of pupils and those concerned with the outcomes of the educational process:

Assessment and the educational development of pupils

- assessment to motivate pupils and improve future performance;
- assessment to provide feedback (to the pupil, parents and other teachers);

- assessment to diagnose strengths and weaknesses so that future performance can be improved;
- assessment to differentiate learning opportunities appropriately;
- assessment to guide the pupil in making appropriate choices;
- assessment to select a pupil for a course, a teaching group or a career.

Assessments concerned with the outcomes of education

- the grading of pupil performance;
- the ranking of pupils against external norms and against each other;
- assessments to identify and maintain a school's standards;
- assessments to evaluate a school's effectiveness;
- assessments to evaluate teacher's effectiveness.

A final alternative definition and associated purpose is obtained by tracing the roots of the word *assessment*. Satterly traces this to the latin *assidere* — to sit beside. If you combine this with *education*, which can be traced back to the Latin *educare* or 'to bring out', *educational assessment* should be seen as the process of sitting beside the learners and bringing out the potential that exists within them, creating an opportunity for them to demonstrate what they know, what they can do and what they understand. Given such an interpretation, assessment in education becomes a positive experience for both the teacher and the learner, a fundamental feature of teaching and successful learning. However, it is important to recognize that although assessment is an essential feature of the teaching and learning process, it should not be seen as an isolated activity, 'a bolt-on extra'. For some time there has been a recognition that pupils, parents, governors, local authorities and central government all have an interest in the assessments that we generate. As Hook suggests, 'Teachers today are being held increasingly accountable for their pupils' progress, and classrooms have become more public places with the progressive involvement of parent bodies and governments in curriculum planning and development' (1985: 4).

In establishing a routine for considering how assessment might become a regular feature of planning for learning, it is likely to contribute significantly to children's progress and also to improve the quality of the learning provided in school as a whole. This was recognized as being of particular significance in the Gulbenkian Report, *The Arts in Schools* (Calouste Gulbenkian Foundation, 1982), where it was suggested that:

> Assessments of pupils are not, nor can they be, statements of absolute ability. They are statements about achievements within the framework of educational opportunities that have actually been provided. In some degree every assessment of a pupil is also an assessment of the teachers and of the school. (para. 130)

The report went on to argue that it is essential that schools need to continually monitor and review the quality of their educational provision and their methods of working, that is, to engage in a process of Educational Evaluation, which is seen as,

> . . . a more general process than assessment in that it looks beyond the pupil to the style, the materials and the circumstances of teaching and learning. If teachers need to assess pupils they also need to evaluate their own practice. Although they have different purposes, assessment and evaluation are obviously linked. Teachers and pupils alike need information on each other's activities and perceptions if their work together is to advance. Assessment and evaluation should provide this as a basis for informed description and intelligent judgment . . . (1982: para. 131)

The report continues to suggest that if we are to regard teaching as a profession, it is insufficient to rely on 'gut reaction' or what we feel to be the case. It is important that any judgments, whether they are about the progress of an individual or about the effectiveness of a school's practice, must be supported by evidence. Before any serious consideration can be given to the organization and structuring of assessment in a school or classroom, it is essential that beliefs, understandings and expectations are made explicit. This is because such beliefs considerably influence practice often without our realizing it. As Sotto suggests,

> We tend to see our practice in terms of our past experience, that is, in terms of a theory we already have. In fact, I think it is safe to say that we tend to view everything we do in terms of an existing 'theory'. How could we do anything, even stretch out an arm, unless we had some kind of 'theory', no matter how tentative or unformulated, to guide us in the back of our minds? In the case of teaching (*or assessment*), our theory will be made up of all our past experiences of being a learner (*and of being assessed*). We will then tend to view teaching (*and assessment*) from that frame of reference, and mostly without being clearly aware of it. In short, our theories tend to come before our practice. And not only do they help to determine our practice, they also shape how we see our practice. (1994: 13, author's emphasis)

A number of writers on assessment argue that a fundamental feature of effective assessment is to have a set of clearly articulated principles. For example, the Organisation Mondiale pour l'Education Prescolaire (OMEP) suggest the following;

- that there should be respect for the individual child;
- that parents should be recognized as the primary educators of their own children, and as partners in the education process;
- that assessment is in the interest of the child and is effected through the child's interests;

13

- that assessment forms part of the on-going teaching and learning process. (OMEP, 1993: 5–6)

Conner (1995) has argued that views about assessment are influenced and informed by particular psychological theories. This is an issue that is recognized by Paul Black, the former chairman of the Task Group on Assessment and Testing (DES, 1988). In a pamphlet written with his colleague Dylan Wiliam (Black and Wiliam, 1998), they make a distinction between a 'fixed IQ' view and an 'untapped potential' perspective.

> . . . there is on the one hand the 'fixed IQ' view — a belief that each pupil has a fixed, inherited, intelligence, so that little can be done apart from accepting that some can learn quickly and others hardly at all. On the other hand, there is the 'untapped potential' view, prevalent in other cultures, which starts from the assumption that so-called 'ability' is a complex of skills that can be learnt. Here, the underlying belief is that all pupils can learn more effectively if one can clear away, by sensitive handling, the obstacles set up by previous difficulties, be they cognitive failures never diagnosed, or damage to personal confidence, or a combination of the two. Clearly the truth lies somewhere between these two extremes. (1998: 14)

The next section distinguishes between the 'fixed IQ' and the 'untapped potential' perspectives of assessment.

The 'fixed IQ' and the 'untapped potential' perspectives on assessment

> By and large, we are still working with models of ability and assessment developed in the first decade of the twentieth century. (Raven, 1992)

At an in-service session on assessment several years ago, I invited a group of local authority inspectors to reflect upon an occasion where they had been assessed, to consider what came to mind and what they remembered feeling like at the time. The purpose of the activity was to remind them that assessment was as much an emotional activity as it was a cognitive one. One member of the group went back nearly thirty years to the time when she had failed the 11+, which she believed had classed her as a failure at the very early age of 11. She explained that most of her effort in life since then had been an attempt to prove that her examiners were wrong in their assessment of her. At that time there was a view that intelligence was fixed and that it was easy to distinguish between children and decide which form of education was most suitable to their capacities. It was grounded in the views of theorists of intelligence whose ideas had been generated at the turn of the century. Alfred Binet, for example, had developed the first successful intelligence test in 1905 to select those children who should be institutionalized, who were regarded as 'educationally sub-normal', 'mentally defective' or 'feeble-minded'! Such views still exist and dominate the educational debate today. Berlak and Newman (1992) and Gipps (1994b) refer to this view of assessment, with its basis in conventional views about intelligence as the 'psychometric' model of assessment. The underlying idea of this model is that intelligence is fixed and innate, that we inherit our abilities from our parents. Since it is fixed it can be measured and on that basis, each of us can easily be assigned to groups, classes, schools and employment. As Gipps suggests, with

> . . . its formulae and quantification comes an aura of objectivity; such testing is scientific and therefore the figures it produces must be accurate and meaningful. The measurements which individuals amass via such testing: IQ scores, reading ages, rankings, etc., thus come to have a powerful labelling potential. (1994: 5)

Berlak and Newman add that assessment procedures are inherently political because whoever controls the assessment process shapes the curriculum, approaches to teaching and ultimately each student's life chances. They argue that,

> Mass administration of standardised tests . . . is largely suited to exercising control from the centre . . . Such tests provide virtually no information about what students are capable of doing or where they may need help. These tests produce relative rankings but little substantive information about what students know and can do which is useful to teachers, parents, prospective employers or to students themselves for making programme or individual decisions . . . The psychometric tradition only enables us to classify and rank students (or teachers) and to constitute individuals as a 'case' — that is, as belonging to a class or category which possesses a particular set of objective characteristics (e.g. high, average or low achiever). (1992: 18–19)

As an alternative, Berlak and Newman advocate the use of 'contextual' assessment which is based upon assessments in the context of activities related to what has been taught, to the skill or idea that has supposedly been achieved. Gipps prefers the term 'educational assessment' which is concerned with 'How well' an individual does rather than 'How many' he or she has got right in comparison to some external norm. Gipps draws upon Wood's (1986) discussion which argues that educational assessment:

- deals with an individual's achievement relative to himself rather than to others;
- seeks to test for competence rather than for 'intelligence';
- takes place in relatively uncontrolled conditions and so does not produce 'well-behaved' data;
- looks for 'best' rather than 'typical' performances;

- is most effective when rules and regulations characteristic of standard-ized testing are relaxed;
- embodies a constructive outlook on assessment, where the aim is to help rather than 'sentence' the individual.

Rather than base his views on dated theories of intelligence, Woods draws upon more recent suggestions which adopt a 'social constructivist' view of learning (Pollard, 1990). The central arguments of this perspective are that;

- learning requires opportunities for the 'active' construction of meaning;
- new learning should be related to and should build upon previous learning;
- learning is significantly influenced by the context in which it takes place.

But what do these claims mean in practice and what are their implications for assessment?

Learning as an active construction of meaning

The term *active learning* is one that is often misunderstood, with the assump-tion that it implies undirected free choice with little consideration of the experi-ence in relation to previous or future learning and an emphasis on practical, physical activity. Accepting a place for activity does not just mean physical activity, it also includes the importance of opportunities for mental activity. Jean Piaget, who is often misrepresented as offering justification for a view of active learning as doing, described two important characteristics of active learning. First, there is physical manipulative experience, learning by doing, and sec-ond, and more important, there is the mental reflection on that experience that allows the learner to reinforce the understanding gained and relate it to exist-ing learning. Views of this kind can be traced back in the educational literature to the writing of classical philosophers. Glaser (1991), reminds us that philo-sophers from Plato to Erasmus emphasized the importance of the role of the learner in the learning process. A distinction was made between *instruction* and *study*. Instruction, which was the responsibility of the teacher, was seen to have lesser value than study because it merely supplied the learner with know-ledge and afforded the learner a passive role. In this classical conception, instruction was insufficient because, '. . . it left too little room for human doubt, inquiry, uncertainty and the search for ideas' (Glaser, 1991: 131, author's em-phasis). There was a place for instruction but it was a subordinate place. Glaser goes on to say, 'instruction should have the mission of making itself unnecessary; learners should become mindful architects of their own know-ledge. The goal of true education was to foster study, or in modern terms, constructive cognitive activity' (1991: 131). This view of learning as an 'active construction of meaning' by the learner is also represented in the writing of current researchers into the learning process. Bennett (1992) comments,

> Recent research about cognitive development sees learning as an *active, constructive* intellectual process that occurs gradually over time. It is not simply an additive process. Knowledge cannot, to use a common metaphor, be poured into learners' heads with the hope that learning will automatically occur or accumulate. Understandings of new knowledge can only take place, or be constructed, in the minds of individual learners through a process of making sense of that new knowledge in the light of what they already know. In other words, learning is a process of *constructing new knowledge on the basis of current knowledge.* (1992: 8)

Jacqueline and Martin Brooks (1993) have attempted to describe the classroom implications of developing a 'constructivist' approach to learning and assessment. In constructivist classrooms they suggest, the pursuit of children's questions is highly valued. Students are viewed as thinkers with emerging theories about the world. Curriculum activities rely heavily on primary sources of data and provide plenty of opportunities for physical and mental manipulation. Teachers seek the students' points of view in order to understand their current perceptions and conceptions and to see where to take them next. Assessment is interwoven with teaching and occurs through observations of students engaged in the process of learning as well as creating opportunities to display the products of their learning in a wide variety of formats.

Learning should be related to and should build upon previous learning

The importance of this idea has already been hinted at in the previous discussion and it also has a long history. For example, Stephen Van Martre, writing in the 1850s commented that the best learning experiences start where the learner is, not where the teacher is. The experience, not the leader, is the best teacher. Similarly, Ausubel, Novak and Hanesian suggest, 'The most important single factor influencing learning is what the learner already knows. Ascertain this and teach him accordingly' (1978). At the heart of these suggestions is the need for teachers to become enquirers into children's understanding of their classroom experiences. The National Curriculum advice on planning in the primary school (1989) described the curriculum in three ways: the curriculum as *planned*, the curriculum as *taught* and the curriculum as *received*. Reflection on each of these reminds us that if we are not clear about children's current understandings and the sense that they have made of their learning, any new learning experience can fall on deaf ears or be totally misunderstood. In this context, it is important not to assume that what a child currently knows is based upon what we most recently taught them. A great deal of learning goes on outside school and children bring well established understandings to their learning in school. There is also a lot of evidence that some of these understandings are wrong. (See for example, the findings of the SPACE project directed by Paul Black and Wynne Harlen (1990) and the study of children's informal ideas of science by Black and Lucas (1993) which illustrated that many children's ideas about science are wrong, but that because they have been established by the children themselves, they are not easily changed by teaching. The only way to move children beyond these erroneous conceptions is to bring them out into the open and subject them to scrutiny.) If we do not attempt to find out what children currently know, our attempts to extend their understanding will be severely hampered. This is why assessment is fundamentally important. Developing ways of getting access to children's current understanding is a crucial element of effective assessment. Since the teacher is closest to this understanding, he or she is in a good position to gather the necessary information to plan the next stages in learning so that more effective learning takes place, learning that builds on and extends the learner's current understanding and competence.

Learning is significantly influenced by the context in which it takes place

The ideas discussed so far emphasize learning as an individual experience, whereas there is evidence which asserts that the context in which learning takes place is as important as the various roles and responsibilities involved. Conner (1992) has argued that context has three important elements, each of which need to be considered when planning learning experiences. First, there is the *physical* context; is the learning environment a welcoming and comfortable one? As adults, a cold, untidy working environment is a disincentive to our learning. This principle applies just as much to children. The second feature of context is concerned with the *affective* side of learning; can I expect to feel confident as I approach new learning? Am I likely to be supported in my learning and can I take risks and learn from mistakes? Or am I likely to be placed in a potentially negative learning situation where I have a fear of failure? The work of Dweck (1986) illustrates the differences between learners in this context. In her work, a distinction is made between positive and negative approaches to learning. Positive attitudes are evidenced by a belief that effort leads to success, an acceptance of one's ability to improve and learn, a preference for challenging tasks, and satisfaction from completing difficult tasks. Those who adopt a negative orientation believe that success is related to ability, satisfaction is gained from doing better than others, and there is a tendency to evaluate oneself negatively when the task is too difficult. An assumption of 'learned helplessness' can become established where any success is attributed to luck rather than effort or competence. Careful assessment enables the teacher to identify children adopting either of these reactions and to modify teaching accordingly. A number of writers have argued that one way of overcoming learned helplessness is to ensure that children understand what is expected of them. Clarke argues,

> Firstly, knowing the purpose focuses the child towards a particular outcome. Very often, children have no idea why they have been asked to do something, and they can only look for a clue or 'guess what's in teacher's mind' as a means of knowing what is expected of them. Secondly, they are being invited to take more control over evaluating their achievements. If the purpose is known, this is more likely to encourage the child to be weighing up the relative strengths and weaknesses of their work as they are doing it. (1995: 14)

The importance of this is also recognized by Black and Wiliam, who argue that pupils can only assess themselves when they have a clear picture of the targets that their learning is meant to attain.

> Surprisingly, and sadly, many pupils do not have such a picture, and appear to have become accustomed to receiving teaching as an arbitrary sequence of exercises with no overarching rationale. It requires hard and sustained work to overcome this pattern of passive reception. When pupils do acquire such an overview, they become more effective as learners: their own assessments become an object of discussion with teachers and with one another, and this promotes even further that reflection on one's own ideas that is essential to good learning. (1998: 10)

The final feature of context relates to the *social* context of learning. For many of us, our experience of learning was as a solitary process with each of us responsible for making our own sense of situations and experiences. Now there is strong support for the inclusion of opportunities to work with and alongside others, peers and friends as well as teachers. Vygotsky (1962) emphasized the cooperative nature of learning when he said, . . . what the [learner] can do today in cooperation he [or she] will be able to do tomorrow on his [or her] own. In support of the thesis, Vygotsky described the 'zone of proximal development', which is, '. . . the difference between what children can do independently and what they can accomplish with the support of another individual who is more knowledgeable and skilled' (Galton and Williamson, 1992).

Again, it is through the processes of assessment that the teacher is able to identify each learner's needs, the support and scaffolding that may be required, and the extent to which they should be given the opportunity to go it alone.

Further elements in the assessment debate

Gipps (1994a) comments that one of the major differences between *educational assessment* and *psychometrics* is a different view of the learner and a different relationship between the pupil and assessor. At the heart of this lies an understanding that performance in any assessment is affected by the context in which the assessment takes place. In addition to the issues listed above, the assessment context includes the relationship between pupil and assessor, the pupil's motivational state and the characteristics of the assessment task. She argues that research on cognition and learning throughout the 1980s has shown that the following factors are particularly significant in affecting performance in assessment:

- motivation to do the task and an interest in it;
- the relationship between the assessor and the individual being assessed and the conditions under which the assessment is made;
- the way in which the task is presented, the language used to describe it and the degree to which it is within the personal experience of the individual being assessed.

'The conclusion is inescapable . . . assessment (like learning) is highly context specific and one generalises at one's peril' (1994a: 5).

Gipps also suggests that in the development of assessment we should 'elicit the individual's best performance' by offering tasks and activities that are,

- concrete and within the experience of the individual;
- presented clearly and unambiguously;
- perceived to be relevant to the current concerns of the pupil and related to recent curriculum experience;
- under conditions that are not unduly threatening, something that is helped by a good relationship between the assessor and the student.

Suggestions of this kind contribute to the identification of principles for effective education systems. As Rowntree has argued,

> If we wish to discover the truth about an educational system, we must look into its assessment procedures. What student qualities and achievements are actively valued and rewarded by the system? How are its purposes and intentions realised? To what extent are the hopes and ideals, aims and objectives professed by the system ever truly perceived, valued and striven for by those who make their way within it? The answers to such questions are to be found in what the system requires students to do in order to survive and prosper. The spirit and style of student assessment defines the de facto curriculum. (1977: 1)

In order for an assessment system to have credibility with the consumers of educational services (i.e., the pupils, the parents and employers) and with those who implement it (the teachers), Nuttall (1987) has suggested that it must be demonstrably sound in a number of ways. In particular, it should:

- be fair and perceived as fair by all concerned;
- be capable of fulfilling formative and summative purposes;
- be intelligible to all who have an interest;
- be economical in its use of resources;
- be acceptable in terms of who controls it;
- be 'methodologically sound', which is usually expressed in terms of the concepts of validity and reliability.

The concepts of validity and reliability are two of the most important concepts in assessment and each of them place conflicting demands on any assessment that is undertaken. Reliability refers to the extent to which a similar result would be obtained if an assessment were to be repeated, whereas validity is concerned with the extent to which the assessment really creates a means by which a particular skill, concept, area of knowledge or attitude is effectively assessed. Most teachers are much more concerned with validity; is this assessment a fair reflection of what the children have been taught? Politicians and policy makers tend to be more concerned with reliability; can I have confidence in these results so that I can compare one result with another? Harlen reminds us that,

> . . . validity and reliability can never both be 100% . . . that we must recognise assessment is never 'accurate' in the way that the word is used in the context of measurement in the physical world. Assessment in education is inherently inexact and it should be treated as such. We should not expect to be able to measure pupils' abilities with the same confidence as we can measure their heights. This in no way makes educational assessment useless. It means that the interpretation of assessment results should be in terms of being an indication of what pupils can do but not an exact specification. (1994: 12–13)

It is probably impossible to create an assessment situation that achieves complete reliability and validity, Harlen suggests therefore that the best one can achieve in terms of quality assessment is the provision of information of the highest validity and optimum reliability suited to a particular purpose and context. Sutton (1990) offers some sensible advice with regard to these issues. To achieve reliable and valid assessments she suggests we need to reduce the main variables that can affect judgments,

> There are three major variables in most assessment by teachers: context (the circumstances of assessment): time (how many times and over what period of time you have to see an assessment criterion achieved); and 'rater' (that is, the person doing the assessment). To put it briefly, do what you can to agree with your colleagues how you can reduce these variables . . . Assessment is an art, not a science, and much of the time you will be relying on your professional judgment and common sense, employing more stringent techniques only when you're in doubt. (1990: 24)

There are two further important concerns that need to be added to reliability and validity, both of which have emerged as a direct result of attempting to implement the national curriculum, those of *manageability* (is the procedure we propose to adopt one that is manageable within our existing resources?) and *consistency* (what procedures are there in place to ensure that our assessments are as fair as they might be?). The most effective strategy for improving consistency has been moderation. Although it can be time consuming, it is the main way in which each teacher can confirm his or her assessment against the views of colleagues. Gipps, McCallum and Brown, reinforce the importance of moderation,

> There is a clear picture of enhanced understanding and practice in assessment . . . All of this has been achieved, however, at a cost to teachers' lives and ways of working. Most importantly, we believe our evidence shows that the improvements in practice, both in teaching and assessing, would not have resulted from the introduction of traditional, standardised tests alone, but depended on a wider approach with moderated teacher assessment at its core. (1997: 6)

Conner has described the benefits of moderation as follows:

- participation in the moderation process contributes to the development of teachers' assessment skills;
- teachers become clearer about assessment criteria and how to interpret them;
- teachers become clearer about what they are teaching and how to teach it more effectively;
- it helps to establish recognized and agreed standards of achievement;
- it ensures that there are common standards and expectations between teachers in the same school;
- it contributes to the development of consistent procedures for marking, and recording and reporting;
- it contributes towards establishing common standards between schools;
- it helps teachers to convey consistent messages to pupils;
- it helps teachers convey consistent messages to parents;
- it contributes to improving the transfer of information from one school to the next;
- it is reassuring and develops confidence in assessment. (Conner 1995: 40)

In addition to improving the quality of assessment, engaging in the process of review associated with the moderation process contributes to improving the quality of education provided by a school. Participation in discussions about assessments ultimately engages teachers in discussion about the curriculum and their aspirations for childrens' learning.

Government advice, however, is concerned primarily with securing standards for end of key stage statutory teacher assessment and pays no attention to the on-going assessments that teachers are making every day in their interactions with children. Yet, these assessments are at the heart of a school's assessment practice. It is these assessments which significantly influence the teaching and learning process and it is fundamentally important that sufficient attention is paid to developing expertise in this area. James (1996) has argued that, government interest is now clearly focused on assessment for accountability and that it is up to schools and teachers to rescue the potential of assessment for learning. At the heart of assessment for learning is the way teachers respond to children — the feedback they provide. This is an issue that has been the subject of recent critical scrutiny.

Formative assessment and feedback

In a study of the feedback process by Black and Wiliam (1998) three main questions were framed. Is there evidence that improving feedback improves learning? Is there evidence that there is room for improvement? Is there evidence about how to improve our skills? The answer to all three questions was a categoric 'Yes!'. Black and Wiliam conclude their review of over 680 world-wide studies of the issues involved with the recognition that,

> ... standards are raised only by changes which are put into direct effect by teachers and pupils in classrooms ... Our education system has been subjected to many far reaching initiatives which, whilst taken in relation to concerns about existing practices, have been based on little evidence about their potential to meet these concerns. In our study ... there can be seen, for once, firm evidence that indicates a clear direction for change which could improve standards of learning. (1998: 19)

An attempt to summarize the important factors associated with feedback identified in the Black and Wiliam study was undertaken by the Eastern Region branch of the Association of Assessment Inspectors and Advisers (Swaffield, 1998). The summary concludes that the quality of feedback is a key feature of formative assessment and that giving specific comments on errors and suggestions for strategies to improve has as great an effect on performance as prior attainment. Successful feedback, it is suggested, needs to include the following features:

- Feedback is more successful in situations requiring higher-order thinking skills.
- Feedback should be related to the task itself.
- As much or as little help as is needed should be given, rather than providing the complete solution as soon as the pupil is stuck.

- Concentration should focus on specific errors and weak strategies.
- Pupils should be offered suggestions about how they might improve, rather than being offered one way of doing something.
- Feedback should be designed so that it stimulates a thoughtful response, building upon previous learning.
- Details of correct answers should be given, rather than just saying whether the pupil's answer is correct or not.
- Comments should focus on progress rather than absolute levels of performance.
- The focus should aim for deep rather than superficial learning.
- Following tests, feedback about strengths and weakness of responses should be given before providing the answers.
- Feedback should help the pupil realize that success is due to 'internal, unstable, specific' factors (e.g. effort), rather than stable 'general' factors (e.g. ability, which is internal, or being regarded positively by the teacher, which is external).

It is also emphasized that some feedback activities can have negative consequences, and that feedback has been found to have negative effects in about two out of five instances.

- Once a gap between actual and desired performance has been identified, feedback should help the pupil find ways of closing the gap and reaching the desired goal. However, other student responses may be that the goal is abandoned or changed, or the fact that a gap exists is denied. All of these can lead to the development of a negative self concept and resultant lack of commitment to learning.
- Feedback which focuses on the self, rather than the task, is likely to have a negative effect on performance.
- The potential positive effects of detailing weaknesses and providing a plan of action for improvement can be negated by an initial congratulatory message.
- The most effective teachers praise less than the average.
- Praise can lead to the perception of success, even if this is unfounded.
- Praise can increase pupils' interest in and attitude towards a task, while not improving the performance itself.

The above recommendations suggest that there needs to be much more careful reflection on the way in which we respond to children and support them in the learning process. This has been the focus of an investigation undertaken by Gipps et al. (1997) which considered the nature and quality of feedback provided by primary teachers to children. Drawing on the work of Sadler (1989) this study emphasizes the importance of the feedback process, in particular how a reaction to children's work can help them to improve on their future performance. However,

. . . when teachers give students valid and reliable judgments about their work improvement does not necessarily follow. In order for the student to improve she must have a notion of the desired standard or goal, be able to compare the actual performance with the desired performance and to engage in appropriate action to 'close the gap' between the two. Feedback from the teacher, which helps the student . . . needs to be of the kind and detail which tells the student what to do to improve; simply using grades or 'smiley' faces cannot do this. (Gipps, 1997: 11)

Over a two year period Gipps and her colleagues have been observing the process of feedback to children by primary teachers. Such feedback, she suggests, has three functions:

- as part of the classroom socialisation process;
- to encourage children and maintain motivation and effort;
- to identify specific aspects of attainment or good performance in relation to a specific task.

It is this last category that is vital for improving the teaching–learning process. The research generated a typology of teacher feedback, details of which are provided in Figure 1.1. The feedback described in columns 1 and 2 focuses on helping children to understand what is correct or particularly good about their work and what needs to be done to improve it. These Gipps describe as *descriptive*, where the teacher describes strengths and weaknesses to the child. The feedback identified in Column 3 focuses on attainment, the specific aspects of successful steps in the learning process, or the identification of mistakes made by a child and how these might be improved. In both of these cases the teacher tells the child. Feedback described in the final column represents a collaboration between the teacher and the child. Teachers using this kind of feedback shift the emphasis onto the child's role in learning, 'using approaches which seemed to pass some control to the child'. It was less of 'teacher to the child' and more of 'teacher with the child'. In particular, teachers in the category described as 'constructing the way forward' provided children with strategies that they could adopt to develop their work and it encouraged children to assess their own work.

The future?

Gipps et al. offers the important observation that, 'Assessment has a role in valid accountability and reporting; but the main role of assessment in the classroom must be to support learning. By developing teachers' skills in assessment and feedback we can continue to build good practice in primary assessment' (1997: 14).

The School Curriculum and Assessment Authority (SCAA) issued advice (June, 1995) which focuses on the need to secure common interpretations of

Figure 1.1: Teacher feedback typology

	Type A	Type B	Type C	Type D	
	A1 **Rewarding**	**B1** **Approving**	**C1** **Specifying attainment**	**D1** **Constructing achievement**	**1** **Achievement Feedback**
1 **Positive Feedback**	rewards	positive personal expression; warm expression of feeling; general praises; positive non-verbal feedback	specific acknowledgement of attainment/use of criteria in relation to work/behaviour; teacher models; more specific praise	mutual articulation of achievement; additional use of emerging criteria; child role in presentation; praise integral to description	
	A2 **Punishing**	**B2** **Disapproving**	**C2** **Specifying improvement**	**D2** **Constructing the way forward**	**2** **Improvement Feedback**
2 **Negative Feedback**	punishing	negative personal expression; reprimands; negative generalizations; negative non-verbal feedback	correction of errors; more practice given; training in self-checking	mutual critical appraisal	

Source: Gipps, 1997: 12

standards across a school. This advice is concerned primarily with securing standards for end of key stage statutory teacher assessment and pays no attention to the on-going assessments that teachers are making every day in their interactions with children. Yet, these assessments are at the heart of a school's assessment practice. It is these assessments which significantly influence the teaching and learning process and it is fundamentally important that sufficient attention is paid to developing expertise in this area. How might this be achieved? What should schools be doing in addition to considering the issues identified above that meets statutory requirements but also promotes the wider intentions of assessment to support and inform learning? James (1996) suggests the following:

- Provide access to training in assessment skills and techniques that will enable teachers to analyse what children know, understand and can do but also gives information about children's misunderstandings and difficulties. This should include opportunities to develop skills of observation and questioning children as well as marking class work.
- Provide opportunities for teachers to discuss children's learning using both tangible and ephemeral evidence. The purpose of such activities will be to agree and check standards with each other and with reference to external materials provided by the Qualifications and Curriculum Agency (QCA). It will also provide opportunities to discuss and share strategies for teaching and learning and to engage in joint curriculum planning to promote continuity and progression. This will create opportunities to build assessment into the planning process.
- On the basis of these discussions, develop a school portfolio of assessed samples of children's work agreed at various levels. This will be a source of reference internally as well as for governors, parents and inspectors.
- Commit some resources to allow teachers to meet with colleagues in other schools to refine understanding of common standards by discussing children's work from different schools. The school portfolio of evidence could be used in this context to extend confidence in internal judgments.

The future of assessment, however, seems to be oriented towards using assessment information more effectively for summative and comparative purposes and in particular to set targets for improvement. This is another central message of the white paper. Paragraph 3.15 argues that,

> The use within a school of reliable and consistent performance analyses enables teachers to assess progress by their pupils and to change their teaching strategies accordingly. Comparisons of performance by different subjects, classes, year groups and other categories help schools to set targets for individual pupils which take full account of each pupil's starting point. Such detailed comparisons also help head teachers to monitor the performance of classroom teachers. (DfEE, 1997a)

In response to the question 'Why set targets?', The DfEE Standards and Effectiveness Unit suggested that,

> Target setting leads to greater clarity and helps a school focus on pupil performance. Head teachers can use pupil performance targets to underline priorities and serve as a reminder of where the school is heading. Target setting also aids school review. Pupil performance targets provide firm evidence against which to judge recent progress. With pupil performance targets, head teachers and governing bodies can see more clearly whether they are achieving or falling short in their main goals. This should lead them to identify the approaches to improvement which work. (DfEE, 1997b: 6)

In a publication produced in 1996 (DfEE), it was argued that the best practice in target setting is based upon self-critical reflection and analysis of a school's performance. All available data should be used to review and monitor past performance and to predict potential performance so that effort and resources can be focused on pupils who are under-achieving or being insufficiently challenged. It is emphasized that target setting needs to be precisely planned, focused on improvement which is attainable and measurable and broken down to a level that allows individual teachers to take responsibility for setting and achieving targets. In a later publication, (DfEE, 1997b) a process for target setting is defined. The procedure that is suggested is framed around a series of questions and has been described as the 'five-stage cycle of school improvement'.

Stage 1. How well are we doing? This focuses attention on an analysis of the school's current performance, by looking critically at pupils' achievements.

Stage 2. How well should we be doing? To answer this question, schools need to compare current and previous results and those from similar schools using benchmark information.

Stage 3. What more can we achieve? The analysis which results from stage 1 and 2 provides the information for schools to set itself clear and measurable targets for improvement.

Stage 4. What must we do to make it happen? At this stage the school development plan is reconsidered and actions identified to make sure targets are achieved.

Stage 5. Take action, review successes and start the cycle again. As a result of the evaluation of the effectiveness of strategies to achieve the targets set, the process starts again and reinforces the importance of monitoring and evaluation for improvements to pupil performance and the standards achieved by the school.

In developing advice for the schools in their authority, LEA advisers in Birmingham have produced a series of supplementary questions, all of which are dependent on the collection and careful analysis of evidence.

Are we doing as well as we should with all our pupils?

What more should we aim to achieve this year?

How does performance in our school compare with national standards?

How does performance in our school compare with the LEA as a whole?

Are we doing as well as schools with a similar intake?

Do we have any significant weaknesses in attainment in particular aspects of the curriculum?

Are there particular groups of pupils on whom we should target our improvement efforts?

At what level should we be setting targets for the core subjects?

At what level should we be setting targets for end of key stage assessments?

At what level should our targets be for particular year groups, classes, groups of pupils, individual pupils?

What process targets should we be setting to develop our whole school systems and procedures for managing improvement?

It is also emphasized that thought needs to be given to who should be involved in the collection of the evidence related to each of these questions; subject leaders, class teachers, pupils, governors, parents? Whoever is involved, the main aim should be 'to improve on our previous best'. As a DfEE document on target setting has suggested: 'Setting targets makes you focus on what children are actually learning, not what you think you are teaching' (DfEE, 1996). Schools that have attempted the process of target setting have not necessarily found it easy. For example, in a report produced for the DfEE (Conner et al., 1998) some of the difficulties mentioned included,

- the fact that as a process it was very time consuming;
- that it was difficult to make targets challenging, meaningful, manageable and measurable;
- that prioritizing was problematic, especially if more than one area of weakness had been identified;
- setting realistic percentage improvements was difficult, as was defining exactly the level of improvement 'wanted' or 'needed';
- it was difficult to involve all children, targeting their individual needs;
- being sufficiently specific about a target was also a problem, so that achievement could be recognized;
- it was recognized that there is a need to handle some issues with great sensitivity, especially when the school weakness pointed to a particular member of staff underachieving;
- the data upon which analysis is based is still relatively crude and focuses on a very narrow range of achievements.

As Barth comments, the assumption that 'strong leadership', 'effective teaching' and 'clear targets' are what brings about improved achievement

... suggests a very limited and demeaning view of both students and their educators. Good education is more than the generation of good scores on tests. Furthermore, what causes teachers and principals to spring out of bed at 6.30 a.m. is not the preparation for, administration and scoring of, and remediation after tests. Tests lead to a preoccupation with production, workbooks, worksheets, and drills, whereas teachers report that the major reward they derive from teaching is promoting, in broader and more imaginative ways, the growth and development of their students ... The kind of school I would like to work in and have my children attend, the kind of school I suspect most teachers and principals would like to be part of, is, in contrast, a place where teachers and principals talk with one another about practice, observe one another engaged in their work, share their craft and knowledge with each other, and actively help each other become better. (1990: 39–40)

Reflection on assessment should be an essential part of the discussions advocated by Barth, and as Swaffield argues in a later chapter, the focus becomes one of assessment *for* learning rather than assessment *of* learning.

A variety of research projects are investigating practice with regard to target setting and the new DfEE Standards and Effectiveness unit is due to publish further illustrations of this in action in schools. It is clear that this is the direction in which assessment is going, and it is important that individual schools begin to take responsibility themselves for analysis of their assessments and to consider the implications the findings have for their children and for their schools as a whole. (The effects that target setting has in Local Authorities, schools and on teachers and children are discussed in the chapters by Dudley and Hewett and Swaffield.)

The major problem with the intensive focus on target setting is that it is emphasizing the summative function of assessment. As James (1998) has argued, the national system for assessment, which was supposed to be based upon the model proposed by the Task Group on Assessment and Testing (TGAT, DES, 1988), originally advocated the importance of assessment in supporting teaching and learning (the diagnostic and formative purposes identified by TGAT). Through successive reinterpretation and redefinition the system has been transformed into one that is primarily designed to monitor standards in schools (TGAT's summative and evaluative purposes). Although not rejecting these important functions of assessment, all four elements should be represented in a schools practice. In other words, the future of assessment should be principally based, containing principles that demand equal opportunity and promotes the achievement of all its pupils. This should be our aspiration for the future.

References

Ausubel, D.P., Novak, J. and Hanesian, H. (1978) *Educational Psychology: A Cognitive View*, 2nd edn. New York: Holt Rinehart and Winston.

Barth, R. (1990) *Improving Schools from Within: Teachers, Parents and Principals Can Make a Difference*, San Francisco, CA: Jossey Bass.

Bennett, N. (1992) 'Managing learning in the primary classroom', ASPE Paper No. 1, Stoke-on-Trent: Trentham Books.

Berlak, H. and Newmann, F. (1992) *Toward a New Science of Educational Testing and Assessment*, New York: State University of New York Press.

Berwick, G. (1994) 'Factors which effect pupil achievement: The development of a whole school assessment programme and accounting for personal constructs of achievement', Unpublished PhD, Norwich: University of East Anglia.

Birmingham Advisory and Support Services (1997) *Standards in Primary Schools: Report to the DfEE on Birmingham LEA's School Improvement Planning Project 1996/97*, Birmingham: Birmingham City Council Education Department.

Black, P. and Harlen, W. (1990) *Nuffield Primary SPACE Project*, (Science Processes and Concept Exploration Project), Liverpool: Liverpool University Press.

Black, P.J. and Lucas, D.M. (1993) *Children's Informal Ideas of Science*, London: Routledge.

Black, P. and Wiliam, D. (1998) *Inside the Black Box: Raising Standards Through Classroom Assessment*, London: Kings College School of Education.

Brooks, J. and Brooks, M.G. (1993) *In Search of Understanding: The Case for Constructivist Classrooms*, Vancouver: ASCD.

Calouste Gulbenkian Foundation (1982) *The Arts in Schools*, London: Oyez Press.

Clarke, S. (1995) 'Assessing significant achievement in the primary classroom', *British Journal of Curriculum and Assessment*, **5**, (3), pp. 12–16.

Conner, C. (1991) *Assessment and Testing in the Primary School*, London: Falmer Press.

Conner, C. (1992) 'Is there still a place for learning in school?', Cambridge: University of Cambridge Institute of Education Newsletter, Spring.

Conner, C. (1995) *The Primary File Guide to Assessment*, London: Primary File Publishing.

Conner, C., Dudley, P. and Wilkinson, D. (1998) *Analysis of the GEST School Effectiveness Special Projects (1b) 1996–97. A Report for the Department for Education and Employment*, Cambridge: University of Cambridge School of Education.

DES (1988) *Task Group on Assessment and Testing: A Report*, London: HMSO.

DfEE (1996) *Setting Targets to Raise Standards: A Survey of Good Practice*, London: HMSO.

DfEE (1997a) *Excellence in Schools*, London: HMSO.

DfEE (1997b) *From Targets to Action. Guidance to Support Effective Target Setting in Schools*, London: HMSO.

Dweck, C. (1986) 'Motivational processes affecting learning', *American Psychologist*, **41**, 1041–8.

Galton, M. and Williamson, J. (1992) *Group Work in the Primary Classroom*, London: Routledge.

Gipps, C. (1994a) 'Developments in educational assessment or what makes a good test', Desmond Nuttall Memorial Lecture, Institute of Education, London, June 10th.

Gipps, C. (1994b) *Beyond Testing. Towards a Theory of Educational Assessment*, London: Falmer Press.

Gipps, C. (1997) *Assessment in Primary Schools: Past, Present and Future*, London: The British Curriculum Foundation.

Gipps, C., McCallum, B. and Brown, M. (1997) 'Models of teacher assessment among primary school teachers in England', *The Curriculum Journal*, **7**, (2), pp. 167–83.

Glaser, R. (1991) 'The maturing of the relationship between the science of learning and cognition and educational practice', *Learning and Instruction*, **1**.

HARLEN, W. (ed.) (1994) *Enhancing Quality in Assessment*, London: Paul Chapman

HOOK, C. (1985) *Studying Classrooms*, Deakin, Australia: Deakin University Press.

JAMES, M. (1996) *The Assessment of Learning*, Unit 5, Open University Course E208, Exploring Educational Issues, Open University Press.

JAMES, M. (1998) *Using Assessment for School Improvement*, London: Heinemann.

LYSEIGHT-JONES, P. (1994) 'An inexact science — issues of assessment', in KEEL, P. (ed.) *Assessment in the Multi-ethnic Classroom*, Stoke on Trent: Trentham Books.

MACINTOSH, H.G. and HALE, D.E. (1976) *Assessment and the Secondary School Teacher*, London: RKP.

NATIONAL CURRICULUM COUNCIL (1989) *A Framework for the Primary Curriculum*, York: NCC.

NUTTALL, D. (1987) 'The validity of assessments', *European Journal of Psychology of Education*, **II**, (2).

OMEP (1993) *Executive Spring Review*. Organisation Mondiale pour l'Education Pre-scolaire (UK).

POLLARD, A. (1990) 'Toward a sociology of learning in the primary school', *British Journal of Sociology of Education*, **11**, No. 3.

RAVEN, J. (1992) 'A model of competence, motivation, behaviour and a paradigm for assessment', in BERLAK, H. (ed.) *Toward a New Science of Educational Testing and Assessment*, New York: State University of New York Press.

ROWNTREE, D. (1977) *Assessing Students: How Shall We Know Them?*, London: Harper and Row.

SADLER, R. (1989) 'Formative assessment and the design of instructional systems', *Instructional Science*, **18**, pp. 118–44.

SATTERLY, D. (1989) *Assessment in Schools* (2nd edn.), Oxford: Basil Black.

SCHOOLS CURRICULUM ASSESSMENT AUTHORITY (SCAA) (1995) *Consistency in Teacher Assessment. Guidance for Schools*, London: SCAA.

SOTTO, E. (1994) *When Teaching Becomes Learning*, London: Cassell.

SUTTON, R. (1990) 'Issues for teachers in implementing national curriculum geography', in LAMBERT, D. (ed.) *Teacher Assessment and National Curriculum Geography*, Sheffield: Geographical Association.

SUTTON, R. (1991) *Assessment: A Framework for Teachers*, Oxford: NFER-Nelson.

SWAFFIELD, S. (1998) 'Assessment and classroom learning, feedback', Internal Paper for the Eastern Region Association of Assessment Inspectors and Advisers, unpublished.

WOOD, R. (1986) 'The agenda for educational measurement', in NUTTALL, D. (ed.) *Assessing Educational Achievement*, London: Falmer Press.

VYGOTSKY, L.S. (1962) *Thought and Language*, Cambridge, MA: MIT Press.

2   Baseline Assessment:
A Case for Civil Disobedience?

Mary Jane Drummond

Introduction

One of the most vivid memories of my schooling is that aged 12 or 13, I learned by heart the first six lines of D.H. Lawrence's poem *Work*:

> There is no point in work
> Unless it absorbs you
> Like an absorbing game.
>
> If it doesn't absorb you,
> If it's never any fun,
> Don't do it . . .

What made these lines memorable was their use by a fellow pupil, Margaret, who had successfully adopted an approach of full-time passive resistance to the teaching and learning of Latin set-books. Through the long hours of Virgil and Cicero, Margaret sat, motionless and silent. It was therefore to her class-mates' extreme surprise that, on the day of the Latin set-book examination, Margaret took up her pen and wrote . . . for a few moments only, and handed in her paper with a flourish. She had, as you will have guessed, presented the startled invigilator with a copy of Lawrence's views on the wrong kind of work, living out in the process his injunction not do to it.

In this chapter, I will argue that many approaches to baseline assessment, past and present, are the wrong kind of assessment. I will urge early years educators to acts of civil disobedience by suggesting that the safest response to this new statutory requirement (in force from September 1998) is, in Lawrence's words, 'Don't do it.' Unless, that is, educators can meet six conditions, six necessary requirements for using baseline assessment in the interests of children. The chapter considers each of these conditions in turn, presenting them as six propositions that could help educators shape effective practice.

The first proposition: Do not do baseline assessment unless you are clear in your mind about the difference between purposes and outcomes. Purposes are nearly always benevolent, or can be made to look or sound benevolent. Indeed, since 1987 and the very first consultation paper on the National Curriculum, and more especially since 1988 and the report by TGAT, the Task Group on Assessment and Testing (DES, 1988), we have been given many assurances about the benevolent purposes of statutory assessment. We have learned the clutch of formal titles for a variety of these purposes: formative, summative, diagnostic, informative, evaluative — all good things for assessment to be (though it is still uncertain whether one form of assessment can fulfil all these disparate purposes). But purposes, like their close friends and relations, aims and objectives, always refer to some possible future state of affairs; purposes belong in the land of good intentions, where teachers write exemplary lesson plans, in the domain of wishful thinking, where we describe the world as we would wish it to be. Purposes are essentially expressions of hope. So it is unwise to judge the worthwhileness of a particular approach to baseline assessment by its expressed purposes. Hopes in themselves have no impact on children's learning; their educators must focus on what does have an impact, and on the outcomes of assessment: what actually happens to children as a consequence of baseline assessment.

Over the last few years, as primary teachers have come to terms with statutory assessment for 6- and 7-year-olds, we have seen this distinction made plain. The *purpose* of assigning numerical levels to children's achievements was to allow comparisons to be made (and more recently, targets to be set). But this same practice had many alarming *consequences*, which hardly need spelling out: competitiveness between schools, early labelling, cooking the books and even teaching to the test.

Another illustration of this crucial distinction is to be found in the notion of accountability. Baseline assessment has been made a statutory requirement to serve the purpose of accountability. But depending on how this concept is interpreted, it will have very different consequences. In one interpretation, accountability presupposes wrong-doing:

> Everywhere accountability is sought, it is the instinct for *punishing and judging* which seeks it. The doctrine of will (and accountable acts) has been invented essentially for the purpose of punishment, that is of *finding guilty*. (Nietzsche, 1968: 53 (first published 1889))

Nietzsche is claiming that people are only called upon to account for themselves when their guilt is known in advance. The consequence of this view of accountability is, inevitably, to be found wanting.

Another view of accountability locates its meaning in the concept of *account* — story, or narrative. This view is much more appropriate for the effective practice of educational assessment. If the outcome of baseline assessment were to be a rich, respectful account of each child's learning, past, present, and in the very near future, it would clearly be justifiable in educational terms. In this interpretation, the outcomes of accountability come very close to the concept of *documentation* developed by educators in the region of Emilia-Romagna, Italy, world-famous for its services to young children.

The concept of documentation is described in detail in Edwards, Gandini and Forman (1993) and by Dahlberg and Åsen (1994); quite simply, it involves making practice visible — to everyone involved, to children, parents, educators and others. As part of their daily practice, the educators use video-cameras, photographs, tape-recorders, huge sheets of paper and precious scraps from children's lives, to capture the quality of life in their pre-school provisions. Dahlberg and Åsen show how documentation is essentially, a process of learning for the educators who practise it; it lays the foundation for development work and opens up possibilities for enhanced communication and collaboration with parents. 'By making the practice visible, documentation can function as a base for public dialogue about early childhood education and care' (Dahlberg and Åsen, 1994: 169). If the practice of baseline assessment can function in these ways, then it will be a welcome addition to effective early years practice. But it will only function in this way if we keep our collective professional eye on consequences, not purposes, always asking ourselves what baseline assessment really does for children, for parents, for their educators, rather than what it is intended to do.

The second proposition: Do not do baseline assessment unless you have, clearly in view, some kind of picture of what it is you want for your children, and what it is you are trying to do in educating them in the years before Y1 and Y2. Put even more simply, this proposition urges you not to begin baseline assessment until you know what sort of children you are trying to educate, until you understand something fundamental about the whole apparatus of education — curriculum, assessment, evaluation; in short, what it is all for.

This condition is, arguably, an easy one to meet, because all educators do have such understanding, though it is often implicit and inarticulate. I have argued elsewhere (Drummond, 1993) that whenever educators engage in assessing children's learning, they draw on an internal value system constructed around their views of what children are and should be. A description of the normal child is not generally made explicit in the process of assessment. Nevertheless, as we set about observing and assessing young children, we do have, deep in our mind's eye, some dearly held beliefs about what we are looking for.

This conviction, that the practice of assessment and the educator's core values are deeply and permanently interconnected, is at the heart of a discussion pack written for early years educators some years before SCAA (now QCA) began to show an interest in children of non-statutory age (Drummond, Rouse and Pugh, 1992). To stimulate discussion about these core values, the pack includes an extract from a fascinating cross-cultural study of young children in pre-school in China, Japan and the United States (Tobin, Wu and Davidson, 1989). In the course of a lively debate about a video-tape recording of a day in a Japanese kindergarten, the Japanese teacher is challenged to justify her treatment of a 4-year-old boy, Hiroki. The American and Chinese educators, watching the tape, see this child as disruptive, difficult, challenging, highly intelligent, but in need of control and constraint. Fukui-sensei, his teacher, and the principal, Higashino stand their ground:

He's got pride. He gets easily offended; his pride gets hurt a lot when we punish him . . . We would only make his problems worse by yelling at him . . . We don't think [Hiroki] is smarter than the other children. If he is so smart, why doesn't he understand better? If he understood better, he would behave better. (Tobin et al., 1989: 22–5)

Under further pressure to explain themselves, Hiroki's educators invoke the concept of *kodomorashii kodomo*, translated as a 'child-like child'.

Over the years, I have found the concept of the 'child-like child' helpful in my in-service work with early years educators, as a way of elucidating their beliefs about children, their aspirations and ideals, their core values about what education can and should do for children. I am arguing here that the effective practice of baseline assessment will have been preceded by some serious consideration of this same concept; if educators are to assess the learning of 4-year-old children, they need to have spent time exploring their understanding of the 'child-like' 4-year-old.

For an illustration of this relationship between values and practices, between beliefs about children and particular forms of provision for them, we may turn to the work of the Steiner-Waldorf kindergarten movement. Educators in Steiner-Waldorf kindergartens in this country have been in the news in recent years because of their opposition to the 1996 SCAA publication *Desirable Outcomes for Children's Learning on Entering Compulsory Education*, in particular to the parts of that document concerned with early achievements in literacy (for example 'children . . . recognise letters of the alphabet by shape and sound . . . They write their names with appropriate use of upper and lower case letters'). These capacities — outcomes or achievements — have no place in the Steiner kindergarten. There the educators use no printed material with the children; they do not require their children to learn either the names or the sounds of the letters of the alphabet.

In November 1996, the Steiner-Waldorf Schools Fellowship contributed to the consultation process on SCAA's proposals for baseline assessment with a carefully argued and principled paper, setting out their position, with particular reference to the assessment of early literacy and numeracy. The following extract from their paper (for which I am indebted to Sally Jenkinson, the Early Years Consultant for the Steiner-Waldorf Schools Fellowship) shows how far the Steiner conception of the child-like child differs from the assumptions underlying the SCAA proposals for baseline assessment.

Our principled approach to not forcing early literacy and numeracy means that our children would be unable to achieve high scores in a baseline test which emphasised the attainment of formal skills. (This is not to say that literacy and numeracy are neglected in our kindergartens, far from it: our children learn all subjects in an integrated way until their second dentition, the time at which formal teaching begins in Steiner Waldorf schools.)

Our kindergarten teachers and parents are naturally concerned that bright enthusiastic children who enter school at five, without having had training in formal skills, run the risk (as a result of inadequate assessment) of being labelled as children with 'special needs'. The 'special gifts' or particular skills they might have acquired in a Steiner Waldorf kindergarten (or elsewhere) would simply not register on any of the tests you propose . . .

Standardised tests provide simple standardised results: their value to the teacher's knowledge of the wonderfully complex and multi-talented school-aged child before her, is debatable. The child is only permitted to show what he/she knows if the skill corresponds to a tick box — one wonders where: 'Can sing beautifully' or: 'Sews with great dexterity and care' might be placed? To put it simply: the scope of the proposed assessments is not wide enough to do justice to the individual child.[1]

I am not suggesting that the Steiner-Waldorf kindergarten approach should be immediately and universally adopted. I am suggesting that all educators would do well to be as clear as the Steiner educators are about their aspirations for their child-like children. I am only too well aware that some baseline assessment schedules that have been published in the past have no such grounding in a principled understanding of children, and children's learning.

For example, the following extract from a baseline profile, devised by two headteachers, and reported in an academic journal, seems to suggest that children are ignorant and incapable, gapingly empty vessels ready for the benevolent input of the reception class teacher (Figure 2.1).

Schedules such as these embody no respectful recognition of the powers and capabilities of child-like children as I have known them. By way of conclusion to this section, the words of Elliot Eisner (quoted by Blenkin and Kelly (1992) in their enormously useful book on assessment) are a vivid reminder of the principle at stake:

Our nets define what we shall catch.

The task is for early years educators to shape their nets, their early assessment practices, so that the most important fish do not escape. With the right nets, they will be able to give a full and respectful account of the fish of many colours who swim so energetically in the waters of the early years curriculum.

The third proposition: do not embark on baseline assessment without being clear about whether you are assessing for divergence or convergence. Are you assessing the ways in which your pupils are all alike, or are you looking for the ways in which they differ? Are you assessing individual free spirits, or potential SATs results? There are important choices to be made.

In my view, a worthwhile baseline assessment schedule would encourage educators to reflect on each child's unique characteristics, on each child's individual understanding of how the world works and what is important in it. Such an approach would support educators in documenting what children's questions are, and their pressing intellectual and emotional concerns. Few of the published schedules that I have collected over the years support educators

Figure 2.1:   Baseline profile

COGNITION

1. Spatial relations(big/little, far/close, heavy/light etc.)
    a) no idea of spatial relationships (1)
    b) makes simple judgments (2)
    c) limited awareness (adequate) (3)
    d) good in specific situations (4)
    e) precise judgments (5)

2. Number
    a) no knowledge (1)
    b) numbers 'parrot fashion' (2)
    c) counts objects to 10 (3)
    d) knowledge of ordinal number (4)
    e) competent handling of numbers more than 10 (5)

3. Colour
    a) no knowledge (1)
    b) limited knowledge (2)
    c) knowledge of primary colours (3)
    d) knowledge of a range of colours (4)
    e) knowledge of colour mixing/rainbow/spectrum (5)

4. Alphabet/reading skills
    a) no knowledge (1)
    b) knowledge of letters out of sequence (2)
    c) phonetic alphabet 'parrot fashion' (3)
    d) recognizes isolated letters (4)
    e) reads simple words (5)

5. Writing/drawing skills
    a) able to paint strokes/dots/circles/shapes (1)
    b) can draw a simple figure (2)
    c) can draw more detailed human figure and other pictures (3)
    d) copies letters (4)
    e) writes simple words e.g. own name (5)

COORDINATION

1. Fine
    a) poor manipulative skills (1)
    b) awkward in manipulation (2)
    c) average/adequate manipulative skills (3)
    d) above average dexterity (4)
    e) excellent (5)

Source: Bensley and Kilby, 1992: 43

in doing any such thing. Some indeed, positively discourage such an approach to individual children, by reducing them to a string of numbers (see Drummond, 1993, for some examples) or, perhaps worse, a string of damagingly judgmental words and phrases. One such schedule invites teachers to assess each child against five descriptions for each of 18 aspects of learning (such as fine motor skills, auditory perception, receptive and expressive language). The instruction to teachers to find the best-fit description for each of these aspects would not be so objectionable, if it were not for the fact that the middle term of each set of five, for every one of the aspects, is the single word 'average', as can be seen in Figure 2.2.

This is no way to do justice to the richness of each child's living and learning, to complex and multi-talented children, as the Steiner-Waldorf educators phrase it. An important example of how to do better has been set us in the work of Piaget, who was not just a great thinker and theorizer, but an indefatigable observer of his own children's learning. For example, he records his daughter Lucienne, at 4 years, 3 months, '. . . standing at my side, making the sound of bells. I asked her to stop but she went on. I then put my hand over her mouth. She pushed me away angrily, but still keeping very straight, and said 'Don't. I'm a church' (Piaget, 1951: 125). Luckily for posterity, Piaget did not practise baseline assessment on his daughter. It is amusing to imagine the result if Lucienne had been assessed on a schedule I have seen that contains an item on how to score children's imaginative play. Here is the criterion to be met:

> Acts out a familiar story, e.g. 'Jack and the Beanstalk/Little Red Riding Hood' or familiar event, e.g. 'Going to the shops' or acts imaginary adventure, e.g. 'Going to sea in a boat'. Imaginary play (sic) such as pretending to be a lion with no development or character, motive or plot is not sufficient to attain the criterion.

So Lucienne Piaget's play, pretending to be a church, with no development or character, motive or plot, is not sufficient to score a point. Fortunately, Piaget's observations were not structured by any such idiocies, and he was free to explain the significance of what he saw in his own terms. The observation is recorded in *Play, Dreams and Imitation in Childhood*, though its French title, *La Formation du Symbole*, is more meaningful here. Piaget's commentary on his daughter's play emphasizes the crucial importance of such early acts of symbolization for later acts of creativity, artistry and authorship. He was prepared to see, in his divergent daughter's play, the significance of intellectual independence and to recognize her powers to think for herself, to represent and express her ideas in ways of her own invention, rather than in ways laid down for her on a pre-formed assessment schedule.

The theme of this section has been the importance of divergence in children, and whether or not it can be represented within the little boxes of assessment schedules that implicitly emphasize convergence. The theme has a particularly topical application in the light of the current political and media obsession with the concept of standards in early and primary education. We might do well to remember how the Hadow Report, the much neglected precursor of Plowden, spoke of standards, more than fifty years ago: 'In none of this should a uniform standard to be reached by all children be expected. The infant school has no business with uniform standards of attainment' (Board of Education, 1933: para. 105).

Figure 2.2:   Best-fit descriptions

Auditory Perception	Cannot recognize sounds.	Cannot discriminate sounds and has difficulty with recall.	Average	Can identify and blend sounds well.	Exceptional phonic blending and recall.
Receptive Language	Unable to listen or remember.	Difficulty in listening and recalling instructions or stories.	Average	Listens well with good memory for stories, rhymes, etc.	Eager to listen, excellent recall and attention to details.
Expressive Language	Poor understanding and use of words — baby talk.	Limited vocabulary and immature speech patterns.	Average	Good vocabulary understanding and imaginative use of language.	Fluent use of language.
Articulation	Does not talk, or difficult to understand.	Many words mis-pronounced.	Average	Clear speech with few mistakes.	Extremely articulate.
Reading	No recognition of sight words or sounds.	A few sight words and some sound/symbol recognition.	Average	Good basic reading skills.	Excellent reader.
Number	Unable to count or sort.	Has difficulty with ordering in series.	Average	Good at number bonds.	Exceptional ability with numbers.
Free Choice Activities	Unable to decide — flits from one activity to another	Often cannot choose, wants what other child has. Has to be directed before settling.	Average	Knows what he wants, settles quickly, inventive and imaginative.	Extremely well ordered and creative.
Attitude to Learning	Completely uninterested. No concentration.	Poor acceptance of tasks and lacks concentration. Is easily distracted, daydreams.	Average	Conscientious, good concentration, keen and eager to please.	Extremely curious and well-motivated, excellent concentration.

The fourth proposition: Do not get involved in baseline assessment unless you have acknowledged the inescapable truth that there is an emotional dimension to assessment, both for the assessor and assessed.

All educators, indeed all adults, have had innumerable experiences of being assessed; we all know, at first-hand, the power of assessment to motivate or to discourage. Many educators are also parents, and from this perspective too, we know something of the emotional costs of assessment, both benefit and loss. In addition, all educators who work or have worked face-to-face with children in classrooms have had opportunities to learn about the emotional price to be paid by those who do the assessing.

One beneficial outcome of the statutory requirements of KSI-SATs (though not beneficial enough to justify the entire cumbersome apparatus) was that the management of this form of assessment enabled educators to see the sometimes painful discontinuity between their own informed, respectful judgments, and those forced on them by the small print in the SATs manual. A powerful example of such discontinuity was shown me by Nargis Miller, a Cambridgeshire deputy head, and I am grateful to her for her permission to reproduce it here (see Figure 2.3). In this science SAT pupils were being tested on their understanding of forces. The rubric for scoring the SAT requires the pupil to use either of the words *push* and *pull* to explain how force can be applied to the teddy bear with go-kart shown in the test booklet.

Figure 2.3: KSI Science SAT testing understanding of forces

Draw yourself making this go-kart move, and explain what you are doing.

One pupil's response, shown above, was highly divergent, and his anxious teacher was not sure he would score according to the scoring manual. She questioned Josh about his picture — had he understood he was supposed to include *himself*, applying force? His reply was to point to the representation of his own hand, on the right-hand side of the picture, doing just as his written text describes: *plugging in the fan.*

Open-mouthed in admiration of this pupil's ingenuity, the teacher nevertheless persuaded Josh to rephrase his explanation to include the all-important mark-winning word *push.* This assessment practice, it seems to me, with its disregard for individual imagination and insight, did violence to the teacher's professional integrity, and worse, to her pedagogical relationship with Josh.

I have used this example, not (just) to demonstrate some of the weaknesses of some of the SATs we have been required to use in the past, but to make a more general point. This is about our responsibility, as educators, to be aware of our power to do good or harm in the emotional domain, whenever we set about assessing our pupils' learning.

Another example of the possibility of doing more harm than good is to be found in Pollard's challenging volume of case-studies of individual pupils in their first three years at school. The illustration in Figure 2.4 shows a page from James' workbook, when he was 4 years, 10 months. We can only speculate about the likely impact of this meaningless task and crushing assessment on James, on his learning, or on his perception of himself as a learner. We can only speculate, but, as I have reported elsewhere, other evidence raises similar concerns.

Margaret Prosser, a primary teacher in Cambridge, was exploring with her class of 8- and 9-year olds, the possibility of constructing a self-assessment

Figure 2.4: A page from James' workbook

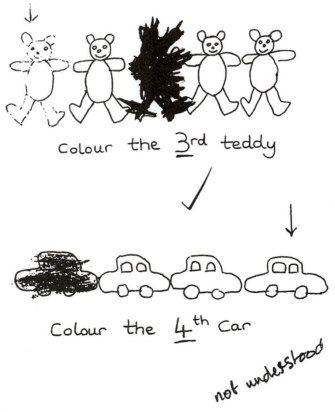

Source: Pollard, 1996: 241

schedule that would help her understand more about their perceptions of their own learning. In the course of classroom discussion it emerged that the pupils wanted their teacher's assessments of them to be kept secret, not to be made open to them as individuals. The teacher asked them why and their replies included the following comments:

> to save embarrassment
> so people's feelings aren't hurt;
> it might be unkind to tell someone they aren't very good at something if they think they are;
> supposing it's someone who is a slow learner. Think how they would feel if you said so.

What is remarkable in this discussion, is not just that these 8- and 9- year olds are aware of the possible emotional impact of assessment; it is that they regard that impact as inevitably negative. There are no references to the motivating power of positive feedback or any recognition of the possibility that the assessment of achievement might enhance children's feelings of success and self-esteem. Their perception is of the potential hurt to children's feelings, and they seem to have excluded the possible rewards of praise and celebration from their account. This discussion . . . suggests some worrying possibilities. Did the pupils' comments mean they had never experienced motivating praise, or reassuring assessments? Were the teacher's comments, her informal assessments, really so hurtful and damaging? How did they know, so confidently, how badly children can feel about themselves? (Drummond, 1993: 137)

In the context of baseline assessments, these pupils' comments must surely give us pause for thought. The questions they raise include: does baseline assessment contribute to children's emotional well-being? Can it be made to do so? And if it can, what must we do to ensure that it does?

The fifth proposition: Baseline assessment has no place in your early years classroom unless you are clear about the difference between learning and attainment, and understand why it is more important to look at learning, than it is to record attainments, or levels of attainment.

There is more than one reason why this distinction is so important for young children and their educators. The first of these is that *all children learn*. Not all children attain some of the specific or specified levels, set down in assessment schedules at the prescribed ages. Some do attain them, five minutes after the test has been completed; some take a little longer — a week, or a year. Some children learn to read at the age of four and some at the age of seven (especially children in Steiner-Waldorf schools). Some do not achieve independent status as readers until still later than that. But focusing on attainment, the end-point of a process, distracts us from learning, the on-going process. Worse, it shows up as failures children who are still learning, but have not yet attained a particular criterion.

Being interested in learning, rather than in attainment, means that educators attend to what happens to young children every day, not just to the children's performances on baseline assessment day in the reception class, or on SATs day in Y2 and Y6. The effective practice of assessment focuses on learning as it goes along, on continuity and progression, not on arbitrary start and end-points. If the practice of baseline assessment leads educators to suppose that their time is best spent in quantifying the attainments of 4- and 5-year-olds as they go in at one end of the infant school, and then standing well back until it is time to measure the attainment of 6- and 7-year-olds coming out two or three years later, then it will be a very damaging practice indeed. Baseline assessment, if we allow it, may cultivate in us a dangerous disregard for the educational quality of children's everyday lives. If baseline assessment practices focus our attention on measures of 'value-added', by inviting us to compare children's scores in the reception class with their scores in Y2 (on completely different criteria, let us remember), we will have lost sight of something infinitely more important than the answer to the value-added subtraction sum. We will be in danger of ignoring the quality of teaching and learning in the years between the two statutory assessment points.

I am arguing here that an over-emphasis on the concept of attainment can limit our understanding of learning. A focus on attainment at some point in the future relegates the here-and-now, the child's daily experiences, to being a means, rather than a worthwhile educational end in itself. Attainment in the distant future is not the most useful criterion for evaluating the quality of children's lived experiences day by day.

Indeed the whole concept of 'value-added' is long overdue for more rigorous critical inspection, not only in terms of its mathematical impropriety, when two sets of scores on two sets of different tests are to be compared, but in terms of what sorts of value educators want to add to their pupils' lives. In my view, effective schools do more than add value to children's levels of attainment. In effective schools, children listen to music, meet artists in residence, visit the sea, climb hills, look down microscopes, and much, much more. They develop attitudes to learning, to themselves as learners, to the world and the people around them, that will carry them into KS2 and beyond as enthusiastic, sensitive, committed learners and citizens. None of these experiences and developments will appear in measures of value-added. On the other hand, when educators are interested in learning, rather than attainment, or value-added measures, they will be attending to just such significant aspects of children's lives.

This is not to say that the use of value-added measures might not have some potential benefits. If there were a way of finding out, for example, whether, as a whole staff group, educators were adding as much value to the girls as to the boys in the school, or to the children who never finish their work sheets or replace the tops of the felt tip pens as to the children who do — *if* there were such a way, (and it is a very big if), and if the taking of such measures did no violence to children or their educators' principles, then there would certainly be a case to be made for it. Nevertheless, the principle would remain that assigning arbitrary numbers to a thing, especially when that thing is learning, can never be the same as understanding it.

In conclusion, I will return to the proposition with which this section began: the importance of the distinction between learning and attainment. Educators who are aware of this distinction, and who choose to focus on learning, will already be accomplished in giving an account of children's learning. Their accounts will document learning that has already taken place, before a child walks through the classroom door, and will detail learning in progress, in the child's first seven weeks in the reception class (the official period by which baseline assessment is to be carried out). These two parts of the account will put educators in a very strong position to carry out their central responsibility: working alongside children, supporting them in their next piece of learning, in the immediate future, in what Vygotsky calls the 'zone of proximal development'. Attending to learning, in short, makes educators more effective.

The sixth and final proposition: Do not start selecting or implementing baseline assessment schedules unless you have already done some work on the principles that will underlie your practice. Do not spend time on practical issues of when and where and how it should be done, until you have in place the principles that will help you answer the more important *why* questions (as in 'why are we doing it this way?'). The principles that groups of educators set in place to guide their practice will be their public justification, their rationale, the external manifestation of their internal value system.

In the discussion pack, *Making Assessment Work*, educators are offered, for critical discussion and investigation, a set of principles that might guide their assessment practices (Drummond et al., 1992). I will not reiterate those proposed principles here, but will focus instead on one principle that I see as potentially extremely powerful in helping us to shape effective practice. In a lecture to the Primary Education Study Group in November 1987, Professor Marten Shipman said, 'There is a close and necessary relationship between what we choose to assess and what we value most.'[2]

This proposition immediately raises some challenging questions. Do our assessment practices in fact focus on what we value most, or on what we find easiest to assess? (How else are we to explain the number of baseline assessment schedules in my collection that record each child's knowledge of the names of the colours, and the properties of a triangle?) What is the significance of the personal pronoun, 'we'? Who does Shipman mean? Who are the educators who will decide what is of most value, of most importance?

In assessing literacy, for example, is it more important to know what writing is for, and to use it to convey and record important meanings, or to use capital letters and full stops in their allotted places? Some classroom examples may help to illustrate how the Shipman principle might read out into practice.

The first example (Figure 2.5) comes from a reception classroom in Leeds, and was given me by Jenny Woodbridge, then an advisory teacher in the city, with a special and well-informed interest in baseline assessment. Laura's writing, shown below (at the age of 5 years, 3 months), will not score many marks on schedules concerned with correct spelling, upper and lower case letters or punctuation. But secretarial aspects of writing were not, at this point, Laura's

Figure 2.5:   Laura's writing

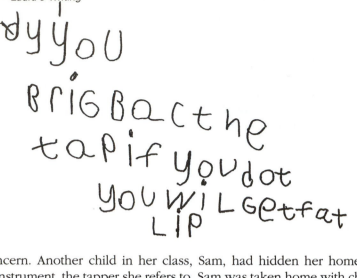

chief concern. Another child in her class, Sam, had hidden her home-made musical instrument, the tapper she refers to. Sam was taken home with chicken-pox before Laura found out about this felony, and her response was to help herself to the writing materials freely available in her classroom and write Sam this far from friendly note, in the form of an ultimatum.

The second example comes from a remarkable infant classroom, charac-terized by its ethos of intellectual search and debate. Liam (aged 6 years, 2 months), noticed that the new three-seater sofa recently delivered to his class-room was being monopolized by some of the children at the expense of others. His solution to this problem (his problem, we note, not one set for him by his teacher) was to take a copy of the class register of names, attach it to a clipboard and begin a survey of sofa use. An extract from the (incomplete) survey is shown in Figure 2.6.

Again, an assessment of Liam's use of capital letters and full stops is in no way appropriate. The SCAA (1997) scales of assessment have nothing useful to say about Liam's learning:

> The child must be able to write at least six words, with at least three letters (excluding the child's own name). The words should be spelled correctly if they are three-letter words. If the words are longer, at least three correspond-ing letters should be in the right order. Record a *mark of 1* if the child meets this criterion.

But I maintain that the Shipman principle accommodates both these children, Liam and Laura, by urging us to assess what we value in their writing. Both of these children seem to me to be acting as literate members of their community, not working towards level one of National Curriculum literacy, but living liter-acy, already well aware of the purposes, audiences and powers of the written word. The Shipman principle, if we choose so to use it, can act as a most

Figure 2.6: Liam's survey

LiOm	o 5 oFFö
Stephanie White	ð
Stephen Heard	ð ð
Isaac Evans	
Reece Bates	ð oð
Angela Boultwood	ð o
Stephen PieKuta	O
Russell Jennings	
Liam Chapman	ð ð
Joe Pluckrose	
Adrian Hewlett	
Joshua Brown	
Sevjan Giritlioglu	ð
Luke Livermore	
Charlotte Marshall	
Rebbie Nagle	
Sarah Parrott	ð
Joshua Barnett	ð
Jade Deller	ð
Katherine Sutton	ð
Steven Downie	
Richie Jeffrey	
Laura Mcleod	
Gemma Whitmore	
Kirstie Peck	O

SoFFo

Liam

excellent razor, with which we may shear off unnecessary and unprincipled practices in our approach to baseline assessment.

Conclusion

If educators can meet the six conditions outlined here, I believe they will be in good shape to practise effective baseline assessment, assessment that meets the most important criterion of all: that is, assessment that works for children. I often speak and write about children's powers, their powers to think, to feel, to understand, to represent and express, above all, to learn. Here I will conclude with a reminder of the equally impressive powers of adult educators: their powers to observe and to respect children's learning, to think about and try to understand learning, and then to make tentative interpretations and sensitive judgments. All these powers will contribute to the effective practice of baseline assessment. It can, and must, be done.

Notes

This chapter is an edited version of a lecture first given at a local conference organized by the Association for the Study of Primary Education (ASPE) in Cambridge in February 1997.

1   For a fuller account of the Steiner kindergarten approach and the fascinating ideas it embodies, see Drummond (1998).
2   For an account of the origins and work of the Primary Education Study Group see Cullingford (1997) *The Politics of Primary Education*.

References

BENSLEY, B. and KILBY, S. (1992) 'Induction screening' *Curriculum*, **13**, (1), 29–51.
BOARD OF EDUCATION (1933) *Report of the Consultative Committee on Infant and Nursery Schools* (The Hadow Report), London: HMSO.
CULLINGFORD, C. (1997) *The Politics of Primary Education*, Buckingham, Open University Press.
DAHLBERG, G. and ÅSÉN, G. (1994) 'Evaluation and regulation: A question of empowerment', in Moss, P. and PENCE, A. (eds) *Valuing Quality in Early Childhood Services*, London: Paul Chapman Publishing.
DES (1988) *Task Group on Assessment and Testing: A Report*, London: HMSO.
DRUMMOND, M.J. (1993) *Assessing Children's Learning*, London: David Fulton.
DRUMMOND, M.J. (1998) 'Children yesterday, today and tomorrow', in RICHARDS, C. and TAYLOR, P. (eds) *How Shall We School Our Children? Primary Education Re-formed: A Radical Agenda for the Twenty-first Century*, London: The Falmer Press.
DRUMMOND, M.J., ROUSE, D. and PUGH, G. (1992) *Making Assessment Work: Values and Principles in Assessing Young Children's Learning*, Nottingham: NES Arnold in association with the National Children's Bureau.
EDWARDS, C., GANDINI, L. and FORMAN, G. (1993) *The Hundred Languages of Children: The Reggio Emilia Approach to Early Childhood Education*. Norwood, NJ: Ablex Publishing Corporation.
LAWRENCE, D.H. (1929) *Pansies*, London: Martin Secker.
NIETZSCHE, F. (1968) *The Twilight of the Idols*, Harmondsworth: Penguin Classics (first published 1889).
PIAGET, J. (1951) *Play, Dreams and Imitation in Childhood*, London: Heinemann.

POLLARD, A. with FILER, A. (1996) *The Social World of Children's Learning*, London: Cassell.

SCAA (1966) *Desirable Outcomes for Children's Learning on Entering Compulsory Education*, DFEE/SCAA.

SCAA (1977) *Baseline Assessment Scales*, London: SCAA.

TOBIN, J.J., WU, D. and DAVIDSON, D. (1989) *Pre-school in Three Cultures*, New Haven, CT: Yale University Press.

3   Out of the Mire: Taming the Beast that Had Become Assessment

Ros Frost

In this chapter, I present a reflection on assessment in my first years of teaching. The chapter opens with a consideration of some of the factors which I believe influence my thinking and practice. I then offer a critical review of one aspect of assessment in my current primary school, our record of achievement, and in the light of that analysis suggest some ways forward, to 'tame the beast that has become assessment'.

Introduction — The mire

My understanding of assessment is set in the context of beginning my initial teacher training in the same year as the Education Reform Act of 1988. In the early years of my teaching I often felt under great pressure from the demands of assessment and in preparation for this chapter, I reflected upon my experience of assessment in the primary school. What have I learned, what works for me and what does not work? These reflections culminated in the analysis presented as Figure 3.1, which captures my experience in three phases; 1992, when I started teaching; then from 1992 to 1995, which illustrates some of the changes in expectation that were imposed upon primary schools, and finally 1995/96 to the present, where I feel in more control. As can be seen, I have presented the factors that I identified as strengths, weaknesses and the issues involved. When I came to label the diagram I found myself stopping short of calling it 'assessment methods', I realized that the 'beast' that had become assessment was actually 'record keeping'. Although this had an important place in the assessment process, it was not what I had seen as the essential element. Assessment for me is mostly about learning, and the ways in which I can use assessment information to help children learn and progress. The analysis presented in Figure 3.1 also identified further issues that were being submerged, in particular the ownership of the learning process by the children. Our Record of Achievement was supposed to be the main way in which ownership was achieved, and I was not sure whether this was actually taking place. In discussion with the school's assessment leader and on the recommendation of an external assessment review, we felt that it would be worth reviewing and evaluating this aspect of our assessment practice. Before discussing how I

Figure 3.1: An evaluation of record-keeping methods used in my own teaching experience

Method	Strengths	Weaknesses	Issues
A – 1992	• helped to focus on learning objectives • profile gave a more complete picture of learning • helped focus reflection on my teaching/pupils' learning • learning logs stimulated communication	• unmanageable • required so much detail they were uncompleted • time-consuming leaving little time to effect planning • meaningless tick boxes	• manageability • nature of assessment • teacher reflection/evaluation • communication
B – 1992/95	• helped to focus on learning objectives • profile gave a more complete picture of learning • provided essential records for reading progress • potential for valuing children's work in own folders • own records very helpful	• unnecessary doubling/tripling up of records • unmanageable • linked to an overloaded curriculum • 'management imposed'/'teacher 'imposed' • did not inform planning . . . or learning?	• links with curriculum • recording • effect on learning • reporting • ownership
C – 1995/96	• more manageable • potential for children's achievements to be valued • linked to a manageable curriculum through short, medium and long term plans • essential for planning /more meaningful learning • effects planning . . . and learning?	• teacher 'imposed' • little time planned for taking RoAs seriously • pupil reflection a low priority	• links with planning • pupil reflection • assessment priorities • RoA • 'assessing' assessment

went about undertaking this, I feel it is important to consider some of the more theoretical ideas that have helped to shape my views on assessment.

Gipps (in Bourne, 1994) pays attention to constructivist models of learning where 'the child is seen as an agent in his or her own learning, actively constructing knowledge'. She also indicates that 'the model of learning which we hold has profound implications for how we teach . . . (constructivist models) being linked with more open and active teaching methods'. She contrasts this with the 'transmission' model and more didactic methods (p. 24).

Gipps also draws attention to the contribution of the Russian psychologist Vygotsky to our understanding of how children learn. First, that 'speech in infancy is the direct antecedent of thinking' and second, that a 'zone of proximal development' exists for children. This refers to the gap between what the child can do alone and what the child can do with help from a more knowledgeable or skilled other. This model can be used to emphasize the importance of interaction between the pupils and their teacher to promote learning. It is in such interactions that a great deal of useful 'assessment' information is generated. This information is fundamental to the assessment process and it helps the teacher to form judgments about each child's learning and progress. Gipps draws on the findings of two major studies; one conducted by Galton and Simon (1980), on teacher and pupil behaviour in the classroom, the other by Mortimore et al. (1988) regarding effective schools. She forms the following statement regarding teacher–pupil interactions from her findings: 'It seems that it is the amount, nature and content of teacher–pupil talk which is crucial to pupil learning and that communicating with groups and the whole class enables more children to experience sustained, higher-order, work-related interactions with the teacher' (Gipps in Bourne, 1994: 33).

I agree with the ideas expressed here and hope they influence my practice. I will revisit them in the concluding section where they help to shed light on my changing understanding about assessment. For now, I return to the decision to review our record of achievement. This next section opens with a brief history of records of achievement, and is followed by an explanation of the evaluation of practice in my school. The chapter concludes with some recommendations for the future.

A brief history of the record of achievement

The Record of Achievement (RoA) was a response by the DES/Welsh Office in 1984 to provide coherence and support for a grass roots initiative. Until this time there had been many different ways of conceiving of assessment: different approaches, (grades, tick boxes, etc.); different emphases, (self-assessment and negotiated methods); and different purposes, (accountability, developing learning, preparation for employment, self-awareness). Yet all of these had arisen from dissatisfaction with existing assessment and reporting methods, (they had my full sympathy!) Munby, Phillips and Collinson (1989: 19–26) list these as:

- *Traditional methods which were often unhelpful,* (i.e., in diagnosing learning needs).
- *Traditional assessment can be narrow and restrictive,* (i.e., reliance on exams).
- *Traditional assessment can fail to motivate,* (it was essential that learner's needs be taken into account i.e., the need to have achievements recognized, feel involved and valued, know what is expected of them and have short term achievable targets).
- *Current reporting and recording systems are often unsatisfactory,* (i.e., in providing a full picture of students).
- *Curriculum and pedagogical reforms and development are needed,* (i.e., to move away from a test-based curriculum and, through the RoA, pave the way for reform).

The DES *Records of Achievement: A Statement of Policy* (DES/Welsh Office, 1984) lists four purposes for the RoA:

1 recognition of achievement;
2 motivation and personal development;
3 to identify all round potential of pupils and see how well curriculum teaching and organization meet these;
4 a document of record.

I began to see the roots out of which our school policy had grown. Yet I was still unclear of the transition between the statements such as those put forward by the DES in 1984 and the introduction of our own Record of Achievement in 1995, over ten years later. What had happened during these years and how exactly had we arrived at our own policy?

The 1984 policy statement by the DES indicated at the time the government's desire to introduce a Record of Achievement for all pupils in secondary schools by the end of the decade. In order to do this the Secretaries of State for Education and Science for England and for Wales felt that further experience of the RoA was needed before a consensus of opinion on the major points of national policy could be agreed and guidelines issued. Nine pilot schemes were set up as a result of this, some in single LEAs and some in Multi-authority consortia. Both a Record of Achievement National Steering Committee (RANSC) and a Pilot Records of Achievement in Schools Evaluation (PRAISE) team were set up in order to monitor and evaluate these. Part of the evaluation remit for the latter was to evaluate how far the aims of the 1984 policy statement were being met within the schemes. Their finding on this matter was that:

> It would appear that the recognition of achievement in records and reports (Purposes One and Four) is a necessary, but not a sufficient condition for the realisation of the core principle of improving learning (Purpose Two). For this latter aim to be fulfilled, process as well as product criteria must be met. If

schools and teachers are not changed by records of achievement (Purpose Three), pupil attitudes are also unlikely to be intrinsically changed.

Broadfoot et al., (PRAISE team, DES/Welsh Office, 1988) within this evaluation team however offer 'a model of the elements required for the successful development of a records of achievement scheme'. See Figure 3.2.

Figure 3.2: A model of the elements required for the successful development of a RoA scheme

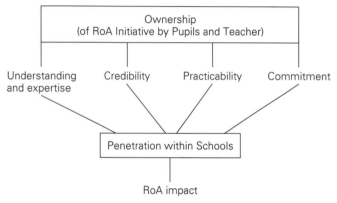

Source: PRAISE team, 1988

Development of understanding and expertise in the processes involved is regarded by the PRAISE team as essential in an effort to provide pupils with the skills needed for self-assessment and negotiation and to help staff break down the assumptions held by pupils about the teacher's role. Questions were also raised with regard to credibility. There was concern that the records of achievement should not be reduced to an elaborate recording process with little change in teacher/pupil relations or ownership and that it should be prevented from becoming just another demotivating influence of little utility to anyone and with an overriding sense for the pupils of being constantly judged. There was also the issue of *practicability* and a call for additional resources:

> To provide for review time and meetings, materials and equipment, INSET, ancillary support and, (in the case of this secondary focus) accreditation. But although such resources may well reflect, they cannot, in any sense, compensate for the commitment of those involved which is, we argue, the ultimate key to success or failure PRAISE report. (DES/Welsh, 1988)

The DES policy statement also stated that the secondary RoA should begin with a summary of primary school achievement. However, the PRAISE (DES/Welsh, 1988) report found little evidence of anything as systematic as this happening. Attention was often placed with the older secondary pupils and worked its way downwards through the school, but there was a desire to extend primary school record-keeping to provide greater information on entry for secondary schools.

In 1991 the PRAISE team produced a *Report of the National Evaluation of Extension Work in Pilot Schemes*. Although its focus remained on the secondary sector it provided a précis of the local evaluation report from Essex, where some primary schools had developed Records of Achievement for primary aged children. Also included in this was a list of areas identified as needing future development, in particular,

- greater involvement of parents in target-setting;
- better procedures for recording extra curricular achievements;
- clearer criteria for the selection of work for the pupil's portfolio;
- discussions on cross-phase continuity in recording achievement.

The report concludes:

> There is every reason to expect primary interest in RoAs to continue to accelerate over the next year or two, driven especially by national reporting requirements. It offers a flexible yet coherent approach to recording development (and potentially, to its reporting) wholly consistent with modern Primary philosophy. If schools are to be enabled to gain maximum benefit from the initiative, it will be important for the Authority to recognise both the variety of needs and practice in schools, and the absolute necessity of supporting their early efforts. (DES/Welsh Office, 1991: 86)

It was from the initiative of this county, with regard to INSET provision for the development of records of achievement, that our school policy was born. I now turn to this in the next section as I consider our current policy and ask whether we are meeting our own criteria.

Policy and practice

The following policy was compiled from whole staff discussion regarding the RoA. These discussions were initiated and guided by the assessment leader at the time who had attended INSET days for this purpose at her previous school. It has been in place since 1994, and as can be seen, there were some ambitious claims.

Record of achievement folders

We need to aim for continuity and progression between years and throughout school life. Our children should be the ones 'in charge' of the achievement folders and should be accessible to them at all times. The folders should also be accessible to visitors through the children. We hope that the children will be proud of their folder and that the folders help to motivate the pupils in various ways. The folders allow the children to participate in recording their own achievements and allow for self-evaluation and for target setting.

- The Record of Achievement folders are started in the Early Years Unit (EYU). From the beginning staff work closely with the children in discussing and selecting work that is to be included, encouraging them to see the progress they make during the year.
- In the infants the children will be involved in setting simple targets.
- In the lower juniors the aim is for the children to be involved in consultations with the teacher to discuss improvements which could be made and to look at progress.
- In the upper juniors the aim is to involve the children in self-evaluation and target setting.

All the children need to be aware of the purpose of keeping the folders (Gallagher, 1994). Yet, how effective is this policy? An external assessment report undertaken in 1996 confirmed the need for a review of our RoA system. My initial thoughts regarding our policy were that its rationale is assumed from the introductory sentences. Why should it work pedagogically? As we have seen, there is research to show that elements contained in the record of achievement ideal have been shown to promote learning. Before I could evaluate the effectiveness of this policy I needed to know its purpose. I read on and found that it hoped:

- to motivate the children;
- to allow for participation in recording of achievement;
- to allow for self-evaluation;
- to allow for target setting;

I then looked for areas where the success of these aims could be measured and arrived at the following which are shown in Figure 3.3. This figure includes the aims taken from the policy from which the indicators of effectiveness arose. From these I formed questions to ask of pupils and staff in order to investigate our current practice, but before presenting the findings of this investigation, it is important to say something about its structure and organization.

The structure and organization of the investigation

My research design is embedded within what has been described as 'the interpretative research paradigm'. As Bassey (1995) says:

> Interpretative researchers reject the positivist's view that the social world can be understood in terms of general statements about human activity . . . [they] recognise that by asking questions or by observing they may change the

situation which they are studying . . . To the interpretative researcher the purpose of research is to describe and interpret the phenomena of the world in attempts to get shared meanings with others. Interpretation is a search for deep perspectives on particular events and for theoretical insights. It may offer possibilities, but no certainties as to the outcome of future events. (1995: 13)

Through holding the above predisposition, and given the nature of my enquiry, I chose to use qualitative research methods. I opted for the interview as my main research method given its adaptability. I wanted the freedom to develop and clarify areas of investigation as they arose, although as we shall see later this caused me problems when it came to analysing the responses. In order to gain an insight into our school's practice through the indicators in Figure 3.3, I decided to interview a cross-section of pupils throughout our primary school and present questionnaires to their teachers. My position as researcher is that I am a main scale teacher at my current school and consider that I am fairly well known to the children by teaching both KS1 and KS2 over the past five years.

Investigation design and administration

I constructed the interview schedule, shown in Figure 3.3, and interviewed pupils from four different classes beginning in the Early Years Unit (4–5 years), and continuing through Year 2 (6–7 years), Year 4 (8–9 years), to Year 6 (10–11). I asked the class teachers to select six pupils; two of whom they considered to be well motivated (Group 1), two moderately motivated (Group 2) and two poorly motivated (Group 3) in order to explore the effect of the RoA on motivation. I then interviewed the pupils in these groups of six. I asked staff not to speak to their pupils about, or add anything to their folders, after I had enlisted their help and before I had spoken to the pupils. I did this in case this affected the internal validity of my research and felt satisfied that this had been respected.

Although I anticipated problems establishing the validity of my data collection I did not realize just how problematic this area would be. In retrospect I feel that the design of the investigation was inadequate in many ways especially with regard to reliability. I had not taken enough steps to combat the potential observer and subject bias inherent in such a project. This may have meant another colleague and I both interviewing the pupils to compare findings, yet this was impractical at the time. As the 'observer' (interviewer), I had taught some members of the Y2 class the year before and found myself gravitating towards unexpected behaviour in children with whom I was familiar. I was also familiar to all of the children as a member of staff and found myself trying to over-compensate for any effect I perceived this might have on the expression of their views. I did this by giving more encouragement to those views I felt were opposite to those which the pupils might have expected

Figure 3.3: *School aims for RoA, anticipated evidence of success and questions used to access this evidence*

School aims of RoA	Anticipated evidence/indicators	Questions asked:	
		of pupils	of staff
• To motivate the pupils	– continuity between years and throughout school life – progression between years and throughout school life – folders are accessible to pupils at all times – pupils are 'in charge' of their folders – folders are accessible to visitors through pupils – pupils feel proud of their folders – the folders help to motivate pupils – all pupils aware of the purposes of keeping folders	(Check to see that policy guidelines are followed in folders) (Check physical access) • To whom do these folders belong? • Can anyone look at them at any time? • Do they have to ask you first? • Are you proud of your folder? • How do you feel when someone asks you to get it? • What is the folder for? • What do you think will happen to it?	• To whom do these folders belong? • Can anyone look at them at any time? • Do visitors have to ask the pupils first? • Are the children proud of their folders? • How do you feel when it is time to do some work on the folders? • What is the folder for? • What do you think will happen to it? • Do you think the RoAs, or their use, need changing/improving in any way? • Do you feel that the RoAs are a worthwhile idea? Please give a reason for your answer
• To allow for participation in recording of achievement	– pupils participating in recording own achievement	• Has it got things in there that you have done well?	
• To allow for self-evaluation	– opportunities for self-evaluation provided – opportunities for target setting provided	• How do you think your work is getting on at school? • Do you need to improve on anything? • What do you need to improve?	• Do you talk to members of your class individually about their work?
• To allow for target setting	– staff and pupils discussing together work for the RoA – staff and pupils selecting together work for the RoA	• Do you talk to your teacher about your folder? • Who chooses the work to go in it?	

me to hold! I kicked myself time and again for doing this as the interviews progressed.

As the afternoon wore on during some of my interviews, I became more tired and less focused, which affected my questioning. I also found myself encouraging more readily those views which confirmed my previously held expectations of how poorly our RoA system was faring. I was aware that I was doing this at the time of the interview, yet I sometimes felt that if I gave no encouragement to express a possibly negative point, it may have kept a valid point unspoken through lack of confidence on the pupil's part. It was certainly a lot more difficult than I had imagined once I came to pick up the pieces in my analysis, hence the number of questions incompletely answered and others which were not part of my original design, which were also incompletely explored. I had not piloted my schedule due to time constraints and so found that, especially with the youngest pupils, I experienced language problems. I rephrased questions to try and make them more accessible, yet found that where I digressed at these points, I left some areas uncovered. However, given these reservations on my part towards the research design, my conduct of it and the incomplete nature of my findings, I do feel there were still some valid points which arose from the interviews.

The analysis

I decided to analyse my data by coding the answers of the children with regard to whether they showed a positive, neutral or negative response to each question. Where the answers were neutral I counted them as a negative response in that they could not be said to show the positive response that I considered an effective policy would engender. Figure 3.4 provides the following kinds of information:

- which questions were asked of whom;
- what constituted a positive or negative answer;
- the amount of positive and negative answers for each area of the policy, to see which areas appeared to be the most and least productive;
- the amount of positive and negative answers for each sex, to see if pupils' responses varied according to their gender;
- the amount of positive and negative answers for each motivation group, to see if pupils' responses varied according to the level of motivation that their teachers perceived they had;
- the amount of positive and negative answers for each age group, to see if pupils' responses varied according to their age.

I hoped that the interviews would shed further light on all of these areas regarding the reasons behind the children's answers. Findings such as these should be viewed with caution and regarded as indicators rather than

Figure 3.4: Pupil response to research questions

The questions (rows):

1. What is this folder for? (can say = P)
2. Who does this folder belong to? ('me' = P)
3. Can anyone look at it at any time? ('yes' = P)
4. Do they have to ask you first? ('yes' = P)
5. Are you proud of it? ('yes' = P)
6. How do you feel when someone asks you to get it? (positive = P)
7. Has it got things in it that you have done well at? ('yes' = P)
8. How do you think your work is getting on at school? (can say = P)
9. Do you need to improve on anything? (can say = P)
10. What do you need to improve on? (can say = P)
11. What do you think will happen to it in the end? (go home = P)
12. Do you talk to your teacher about your folder? ('yes' = P)
13. Who chooses the work to go in it? ('me'/'me' + teacher = P)
14. Does the RoA help your learning? ('yes' = P)
15. Do the 'learning logs' help your learning? ('yes' = P)
16. Do you enjoy working on your RoAs? ('yes' = P)
17. What would you like to happen to your folder in the end?

Column headers: E Y U (Intv.2nd) | Y R 2 (Intv.3rd) | Y R 4 (Intv.1st) | Y R 6 (Intv.4th) | P N

Annotations in table: "Rephrased and asked as Q4", "Rephrased and asked as Q16"

Number of answers:	Girls	Boys		Group 1	Group 2	Group 3
Positive	75	76		54	49	48
Negative	24	26		13	17	20

P = Positive   N = Negative   H = Home   S = School   B = Boy   G = Girl
1 = perceived as well motivated by class teacher
2 = perceived as fairly motivated by class teacher
3 = perceived as poorly motivated by class teacher

Dark grey = (P) Question asked and answered in a positive manner
Light grey = Question asked but answered in a negative or neutral manner
White = Question not asked

60

certainties for some of the following reasons; I may not have asked the right questions to get access to the information I needed, i.e., Does talking to the teacher about their folders constitute target setting? Did inappropriate wording of questions hinder the understanding of the youngest children in the Early Years Unit (EYU), especially one of the pupils whose first language was French, even though he communicates well in English. He gave a majority of neutral answers throughout the interview, which with hindsight indicated to me his need for language support in this session.

Findings

In general:

- Two-thirds of all responses were of a positive nature;
- Boys and girls responded with similar amounts of positive and negative answers;
- Those who were perceived by their teachers as being well motivated in their work made the most positive comments followed by fewer positive answers as the motivation of the pupils decreased.

Continuity and progression:

- All ages used the parts of the RoA appropriate to their age group and in keeping with the agreed policy on when they should be used.

Accessibility:

- All folders were physically accessible to all the children. Y2, 4 and 6 collected their own folders. Due to a temporary obstacle the EYU pupils' folders were collected by their teacher on the day I interviewed them.

Ownership:

- 54 per cent of the 24 pupils asked knew that the folder belonged to them. The remaining pupils, (all of the Y4 pupils and a mix of EYU and Y2 pupils) thought that the folders belonged to the school. All members of staff said that the folders belonged to the children, with an element of class ownership at Y4.
- 78 per cent of the pupils expected a visitor to ask their permission before seeing their folders. All of the teachers of the pupils asked also expected visitors to ask the pupils' permission. One of the youngest pupils displayed a strong sense of ownership in this area, as can be seen from the following extract from our discussion;

> *T:* And Z? Would I have to ask you after I'd asked Mrs. A?
>
> *Z:* Ask Mrs. A.
>
> *T:* And then do I have to ask you?
>
> *Z:* Yes.
>
> *T:* Why is that?
>
> *Z:* Because it's my folder. (Group 3 pupil in EYU)

- 22 per cent did not expect to be asked — who were they? The French pupil in the EYU plus half of the pupils in Y4 who had been placed in groups 2 and 3 for motivation. I wondered if there was any link here between pupils who are perceived to be poorly motivated and a lessening in the say of who handles their work. A similar concern crossed my mind when considering who chose work for their folders as it was a group 3 pupil in Y2 who said that they did not participate in choosing their work. However, these are purely hypotheses and are based on minimal grounds. They would need further exploration to see if there is any weight in them at all.

- 8 per cent of the pupils could say that their folders went home in the end. Clearly it is of great concern that 92 per cent of pupils (while able to give good reasons as to where it might go), were unable to say that the RoAs went home with them for sure in Y6. The 8 per cent who answered positively were in the EYU. I wondered how much of this was to do with certainty of destiny or the apparent desire of this age group to take everything home! All of the teachers asked were also unsure (as I was at the outset of this project). I wondered how many of us would put so much effort into something with such an uncertain ending.

Pride in folders:

- 89 per cent of the pupils were proud of their folders. All members of staff, except in Y6, perceived their pupils to be proud of them too. It was felt by the Y6 teacher that its poor format did not encourage pride, a perception supported by this Y6 pupil;

> *T:* OK. S. How do you feel when you're asked to get it (the folder)?
>
> *S:* Oh it's a really stupid reason but I don't like the front cover of it. I think it's really awful so I don't like getting it out because of that. (Y6 pupil — group 1)

The following comment however shows the reason why one Y4 pupil is proud of his folder;

> *T:* G. Are you proud of your folder?
>
> *G:* Yes I'm very proud of it.
>
> *T:* Would you like to show me your folder . . . the bits you're proud of?

G: Err . . . (flicks through pages) I'm proud of the d_____(?) poem because it took . . . mm . . . because it took quite a long time and I got it all done in the end.

T: Right, so you tried very hard with that one?

G: Yes. (Y4 pupil — group 3)

Of the remaining 11 per cent who were counted as 'not proud of their folders' one of these answers was neutral, possibly through language difficulties, and the other was made by the following 'well motivated' pupil who gave a majority of negative answers.

T: D. Are you proud of your folder?

D: Not at all.

T: Not at all! Why is that?

D: Because I hate handwriting.

T: Is there a lot of handwriting?

D: Um, yeah. (Y4 pupil — group 1)

- All of the pupils said that their folders contained work that they had done well at.

- 82 per cent of the pupils said that they wanted to take their folders home and that their parents would praise them for the good work they had done. The remaining 18 per cent included 1 undecided pupil and 3 pupils who wanted their work either to stay at their present school or go on to their next school so that people could see what their work was like.

Motivation:

- 22 per cent of the pupils enjoyed working on their folders. It appeared that those who were already motivated to work enjoyed this as they would any other activity (those who answered positively were in the top motivational group). However, even within this group comments such as the following were made;

T: Do the Records of Achievement help?

S: . . . no not really, 'cause I don't know what happens to them when you finished . . . why do you need to put on pieces of work you've done about why you're pleased with them? You're going to take them home with you anyway, so I just don't see why. (Y6 pupil — group 1)

I question whether we sometimes lean too heavily on written work and recording in our RoAs thus making them demotivating by their tediousness. The PRAISE (DES/Welsh Office, 1988: 171) report also makes this similar observation:

How can schools work to prevent records of achievement being reduced simply to an elaborate recording process?

- The 78 per cent who did not enjoy working on the folders made comments such as the following;

    T: OK. Y. How do you feel when you have to get your folder?
    Y: Sad.
    T: Sad? . . . Why's that?
    Y: Because it's boring.
    T: Because it's boring? . . . Why is it boring?
    Y: Because you have to do lots and lots of hard work.

    This was contradicted by another child who said

    T: M. How do you feel when you get your folder?
    M: Happy.
    T: Why is that?
    M: 'Cause I like doing work. (Two EYU pupils — group 1)

- Two thirds of the 6 Y6 pupils asked said that they felt that the RoA did help their learning. Of the third who did not think like this, the replies came from the less motivated pupils.

Learning Logs: (These are individually completed by the children and provide an opportunity for them to comment to their teacher about their learning and any successes or difficulties that they have experienced.)

- Two-thirds of the six Y6 pupils said that they felt that the Learning Logs helped their learning, this was expressed in the following ways;

    P: Sometimes I like doing them 'cause if I've fallen out with my friend I can tell Mrs B. It just helps to tell somebody. (Y6 pupil — group 2)

    Another child commented,

    L: Well I don't really like writing in them but they can help you, . . . when you fall out with friends and you can write something private in there about it and Mrs B. sometimes replies back and tells you what to do or something. (Y6 pupil — group 3)

- Of the third who did not feel that writing in their learning logs helped them, the replies came from the children identified as being most highly motivated. The following were reasons expressed:

    F: Well I never have anything to say really because . . . I think that maybe we should have them when you wanted, write something when you really want to, and give them in maybe every week.
    T: How often do you do them, every week?
    F: Every Friday. I think it's a bit too often . . . (Y6 pupil — group 1)

- Another child questioned their use because she had not received a response to an issue that she had raised:

  > *S:* I don't like writing in them ... I've asked Mrs. B something for two weeks and she hasn't written a reply or anything in it so it's a waste of time. (Y6 pupil — group 1)

- I thought of the original reasons we had identified for introducing the Learning Logs (given in the last Assessment Review by the school's Assessment leader):

  > ... staff felt that progressing to the use of an ongoing Learning Log and the setting of regular targets by the children themselves would provide a more thought provoking process of self-evaluation and hence lead to improved self assessment when selecting work to be kept. (Lawler, 1996)

I questioned whether the above aims had been met. It seemed to me from the interviews that the process had become trivial and laborious for most of the pupils asked. While there appear to be great personal and social benefits to the Learning Logs I am not sure that they are helping pupils develop the self-evaluation we hoped for. I was also very concerned that we might be overloading staff with written communication that is impossible to manage. Can a teacher be expected, on top of marking, to maintain a meaningful written dialogue each week with 32 individuals?

Purpose of keeping the folder

- 67 per cent of the pupils knew what the folder was for, they gave reasons such as:

  > *T:* B. What are these folders for?
  > *B:* You can look back at what you done last year and the year before that.
  > *T:* OK and why do you do that?
  > *B:* To remember what you did last year and see if you've done it any better. (Y2 pupil — group 1)

  > *T:* S. what's it for?
  > *S:* (laughing) Well you can put personal information in and stuff so, who are your friends and things and you can also colour in what you can do and what you can't.
  > *T:* OK, and H?
  > *H:* It's really the same as S. but you can put everything in and it makes you feel really good about yourself too.
  > *T:* OK ... Why does it make you feel good about yourself?
  > *H:* Well you can see how much you've improved and what you can do now that you could't do before. (Y6 pupil — Group 2)

Of the third who were not sure it was the pupils from the EYU and two from Y4.

T: OK. R. What do you think it's for?
R: You.
T: For me? Thank you! L. What do you think it's for?
L: Colouring. (EYU pupils — Groups 2 and 3)

This illustrates both the language problems I experienced and also the question of what kind of meaning we can expect young pupils to make of the RoA. How can such meaning go beyond colouring to beginning to develop their ideas of pride, quality and progression?

The teachers asked all felt that the RoA was worthwhile. They justified the effort invested in the folders as enabling; 'reflection on achievement', 'reflective learning', 'children to see progress' and 'move on to new targets'. In KS2 there was more of an emphasis on it being a 'record of children's work and achievement' yet 'designed for children's self motivation, self worth and personal evaluation'.

Participation in choosing own work:

- Two-thirds of the pupils helped to choose the work to go into their folder. Those who did not belonged to the EYU and one Y2 pupil in group 3.

Evidence of self-evaluation:

- 90 per cent of the pupils could say how they thought their work was progressing. The remaining 10 per cent were pupils in Y4 whose responses in the main had been neutral or negative. It was impossible to say at the time why their replies were as such.
- All of the pupils could say *if* they needed to improve on anything.
- All of the pupils could say *what* they needed to improve on.

Evidence of target setting:

- All of the pupils said that they talked to their teachers about their folders and discussed ways that they could improve.

Suggestions for change and improvement

The pupils and staff were very forthcoming with ideas for how the folders could be improved. Listening to the children and their ideas seems fundamentally important to overcome the concerns voiced in the PRAISE report (DES/Welsh Office, 1988: 76)

How can the situation be avoided in which the record of achievement becomes just another demotivating influence for some pupils, a school-imposed and controlled procedure that serves only to record their relative lack of progress compared to other pupils — a procedure which engenders no sense of ownership, either of process or product?

To summarize, this small scale investigation revealed that we have a great deal to be pleased with such as:

- the immense pride of most of the children in their good work folders;
- the majority of pupils understand the use of their folders;
- the self-reflection that is taking place through discussion with teachers;
- the number of pupils who choose their own work for their folders;
- the positive perception by the pupils of their parents' interest in their achievements;
- continuity and progression of the material in the folders themselves, as can be seen by comparison from one year to the next;
- the accessibility of the folders;
- the staff commitment to the initiative.

There are also points which need addressing:

- ownership and destination of the folders;
- greater clarity and communication of purpose;
- the demotivating nature of 'working on' the RoAs;
- selection of more of the children's own work for folders and whether it should be original or photocopied;
- more presentable format;
- more interesting/interestingly presented contents/sheets;
- differentiation;
- adequate time to use RoAs and Learning Logs effectively.

If we consider the PRAISE model for successful development of RoAs in schools, we can see that we have concerns regarding ownership, credibility and practicability with some minor developments needed in understanding and expertise. Fortunately the one thing that neither staff nor pupils are short on is commitment! In the final section I suggest ways to develop these weaknesses into strengths.

The way forward?

Although the aims of our Record of Achievement policy are illustrated in our practice, I would argue that it suffers from a low status. At the heart of our policy are the desires to motivate, record achievement and allow for self-evaluation and target setting. If we look back to the findings of Galton and

Mortimore and the contributions of Vygotsky discussed earlier, it becomes easier to see the necessity of high quality and sustained teacher–pupil interaction as a way of promoting the development we desire. I would suggest that the low status it has at present is due to the following reasons, the first two of which reflect the results of the investigation:

- too little time for high quality and sustained teacher–pupil interaction;
- poor presentation and format;
- a reliance on written evaluation and recording in the absence of meaningful dialogue;
- lack of clear purpose/destination/ownership.

So, where do we go from here? In the light of this research initiative, I have suggested the following aims for the future. The advice of Shearer and James (1988) provides an important starting point,

> Where pupils had received summative documents, it was evident that they were impressed by the quality of the product. Moreover, this appeared to be having a positive effect on the value they attached to the work that went into its production. The growing consensus in schools was that the final document should be attractively produced and presented to pupils at formal occasions which give them status. (Shearer and James, 1988: 24)

In the light of the above statement, I recommended that we introduce a 'This is your life' presentation to pupils in Y6 with their folders a record of their development and achievement while at our school. This event would be clearly communicated to other pupils as the purpose and destination of their good work folders.

In order to have a folder worthy of such a presentation I proposed consultation with members of the pupil's school council and the assessment leader regarding changes to the presentation and format of the folders. I recommended that pupils choose more of their own work, after receiving advice on appropriate criteria for selection, and are invited to say whether they would like original or photocopied work included. It was also suggested that more attention should be paid to lessening the amount of recording required.

With the format of the folders revitalized I suggested the establishment of fortnightly review meetings between small groups of pupils and their teachers, aiming to see each pupil once per term. In order to do this the weekly 'PSE/ circle time' could be moved to a fortnightly space which would mean reviews and circle times taking place on alternate weeks. In preparation the pupils would choose work to bring to these meetings thus giving relevance to the 'work sample information' sheet that we had developed. Pupils could use this to prepare for sharing their achievements with the other pupils and their teacher. It was also suggested that an achievement folder should be kept in each class for children to record independently in words, pictures or photocopies their achievements at the time that they happen. This too could be brought to the review meeting and discussed.

I recommended that there should be a standard format to the review times where pupils have a time to present their work and the others take it in turns to comment positively on it and/or ask questions about it. Johnson, Hill and Tunstall in their work on the primary Records of Achievement also advocate the inclusion of this essential ingredient: 'The development of children's ability to recognise and share achievements depends upon the ethos of the class and the sensitivity to the need in others for recognition and praise' (1992: 20). The rules, from Bliss and Tetley (1993) and sanctions governing our 'circle times' should be promoted during this time. They are as follows:

- We listen when someone else is speaking.
- We may pass.
- We do not remind anyone else what they should be doing.
- There are no 'put downs'.
- Three warnings and then removal from group to deal with abuse of these rules.

I consider that such a focus would allow higher quality and more sustained interaction between the pupil and teacher. From their research as members of the PRAISE team Shearer and James found this to be beneficial. 'On the whole pupils valued opportunities to discuss their progress with teachers on a one-to-one basis. If anything though teachers valued them even more' (1988: 24). I also argued that our marking policy should act as the guideline for most of our pupil and teacher reflection on curriculum areas and regular target setting. This would leave review times free for pupils to set their own targets in a more meaningful way that would not suffer from 'overkill'. I recommended that Learning Logs be reviewed in greater depth regarding pupil and staff views.

I also considered it important that we look further into continuing the links established with parents in the EYU, where parents are invited to provide information about their child's achievements before they start school (and for these documents to go into their RoAs). Given that the children have so much faith in their parents' encouragement, I think we would be foolish to leave such a potential source of support unregarded.

These are the ways in which we are now attempting to improve our Record of Achievement and to take back some control of the assessment process that is more in accord with our views about learning. It remains to be seen whether, over the coming months, we are able to yield a rich harvest.

References

BASSEY, M. (1995) *Creating Education Through Research*, Edinburgh: Kirklington Moor Press in conjunction with BERA.

Bliss, T. and Tetley, J. (1993) *Developing Circle Time*, Bristol: Lame Duck Publishing.

Bourne, J. (1994) *Thinking Through Primary Practice*, London: Routledge.

Broadfoot, P., James, M., McMeeking, S., Nuttall, D. and Stierer, S. (1988) Records of Achievement: Report of the National Evaluation of Pilot Schemes, London: HMSO.

DES/Welsh Office (1984) *Records of Achievement: A Statement of Policy*, London: HMSO.

DES/Welsh Office (1988) *Report by the Pilot Records of Achievement in Schools Evaluation (PRAISE) Team — Records of Achievement: Report of the National Evaluation of Pilot Schemes*, London: HMSO.

DES/Welsh Office (1991) *Report by the Pilot Records of Achievement in Schools Evaluation (PRAISE) Team — Records of Achievement: Report of the National Evaluation of Extension Work in Pilot Schemes*, London: HMSO.

Gallagher, L. (1994) *Record of Achievement Policy*, Mersea Island School (GM): Essex.

Galton, M. and Simon, B. (1980) *Progress and Performance in the Primary Classroom*, London: Routledge and Kegan Paul.

Johnson, J., Hill, B. and Tunstall, P. (1992) *Primary Records of Achievement: A Teachers' Guide to Reviewing, Recording and Reporting*, London: Hodder and Stoughton.

Lawler, J. (1996) *Assessment Report*, Mersea Island School (GM): Essex.

Mortimore, P., Sammons, P., Stoll, L., Lewis, D. and Ecob, R. (1988) *School Matters. The Junior Years*, Wells, Somerset: Open Books.

Munby, S., Phillips, P. and Collinson, R. (1989) *Assessing and Recording Achievement*, Oxford: Blackwell.

School Examinations and Assessment Council (1990) *Records of Achievement in Primary Schools*, London: HMSO.

Shearer, B. and James, M. (1988) 'Souvenirs of schooldays' in *Times Educational Supplement*, 25.11.88, p. 24.

4   The Role of Target Setting in School Improvement: An Illustration in the Context of the Leys Primary School

Philip Hewett

Introduction

Let me say straight away that target setting is not an overall panacea for the improvement of schools. If governors and headteachers simply say to their staff you must work harder in order to achieve x per cent improvement in SAT scores, or whatever other aspect of school life is being targeted for improvement (and one hopes there will be some, for example PSHE (Personal, Social and Health Education), or PE given the overall level of fitness of our nation's youth) then target setting is a short route to a nervous breakdown for all concerned! In order to make improvements you have to do something different. It may or may not be dramatic, but it has to be sufficient for you to believe that it may bring about an improvement. You then set the target and it is the initiative that is then under pressure and succeeds or fails, not individual members of staff.

There is no short cut to the process of school improvement planning that we have all been engaged in for some years. We still need to analyse where we are, where we want to go, and how we are going to get there. We then review and start all over again. I make no apology for using the word 'we' so many times, as it is important to remember school improvement cannot be achieved unless everyone is able to feel some sense of ownership. The difference in recent years is that we now have so much data about national averages, and county averages, and peculiar beings such as 'pixies' and 'pandas' that we are also able to feed into the process comparisons with other schools.

At the time of writing this chapter we are being told that we are able to compare ourselves with similar schools through the 'panda'. However, in my view, pandas have not been produced in nearly enough detail to provide helpful comparisons. Pandas divide schools into two groups: those with 50 per cent or more ethnic minorities and those with less than 50 per cent. These two groups are then sub-divided according to the percentage of free school meals. There is an enormous amount of difference between schools that have 0 per cent ethnic minorities on roll and a school that has 50 per cent. This is not to mention which ethnic minority, economic background, refugee status, etc. Free school meals is also a crude measure covering a multiplicity of circumstances. It is now clearly established that the most reliable determinant of future achievement is prior achievement. Depending on the key stage, we may be talking about baseline, or previous National Curriculum assessments. This has, therefore, been the key measure that we have used when setting targets. However, as I will show, comparisons with county and national averages have been important for determining how successful we are being when comparing achievement in different core subjects, and despite my earlier disparaging comments, it also helps to know where the school fits within the overall range of achievement of schools both locally and nationally even if direct comparisons are difficult.

It is my belief that school improvement needs to be approached in a holistic manner, involving all the people who collectively make up the community that is the school. Similarly the most important determinants of success or failure are the relationships between those people. If we have achieved a measure of success at The Leys it is because everybody associated with the school has worked together as a team, staff, governors, parents, the LEA, and most importantly the children who wanted to feel good about themselves and take a pride in the school. Different groups and different individuals have all been responsible for a variety of initiatives that have contributed to achieving our aims. In this chapter I will attempt to show how target setting has provided a focus for key aspects of the school improvement plan and has followed both an analysis of where the school needed to improve and carefully thought through curriculum initiatives which might bring about that improvement. I will also attempt to show how an analysis of data over time helps to make target setting realistic, and provides a powerful tool for making judgments about areas of strength and weakness.

Target setting has been one means by which we have achieved a collective focus. However, in order to appreciate the role of target setting it is important to have a brief understanding of the context in which it took place and the collection of initiatives which all contributed to the impetus for raising standards in all aspects of school life.

The context (where we were)

The Leys Primary School was formed in April 1993 from the amalgamation of two former schools which shared the same site. One was an infants with a nursery, and the other a juniors with an EBD unit. Both schools had been going through a bit of a rough patch — the juniors had four headteachers in the previous five years (two acting) and a drop in numbers between both nursery and infants and infants and juniors. The schools were still viable but the governors decided that it made sense to amalgamate for a variety of reasons which included the desire to relaunch the school with a fresh name. I was appointed as headteacher of the new school to bring about the amalgamation.

In Hertfordshire terms the school serves a relatively needy area with over 30 per cent of children receiving free school meals. Approximately 10 per cent of children are from ethnic minorities, and a significant minority of families are in temporary accommodation. A Stevenage Borough Council survey undertaken in 1993 identified the St Nicholas area of Stevenage, which our school serves, as being the area where people least liked to live. Local residents had a poor sense of self-esteem and there were high levels of long term unemployment and nuisance crime, such as vandalism. The school was a particular target for vandalism, which on average cost between £4000 to £6000 a year. The area lacked a focal point to establish a sense of community.

The junior school troubles could be traced to the time when, five years before the amalgamation, an EBD unit catering for the needs of eight seriously disturbed youngsters was transferred to a spare classroom in the school. The head who agreed to take the unit was at the same time asked to take over another local school on a caretaker basis and was later appointed to the job permanently. The children from the unit caused serious problems at playtimes and dinner times, with violent and uncontrolled behaviour. There were also difficulties integrating the work of the unit with the remainder of the mainstream school. The school began to get a reputation for having unruly pupils and as a result some parents chose to send their children elsewhere when they had completed their infant schooling. Lunch-time behaviour was also clearly identified by staff, parents and governors as the major problem at the infants school. The nursery was well regarded but a number of parents who witnessed the poor behaviour decided that their children would not transfer to the infants.

In addition to these problems, a substantial minority of parents felt alienated and said they found it difficult to talk to the teachers. There was a high level of pupil absence in both schools (nearly 10 per cent) and during the last full year of the infant school there had been very low National Curriculum results (only 40 per cent of children had achieved Level 2).

Both schools benefited from experienced staff, both teaching and nonteaching, who were committed, hard working, enthusiastic and ready for change. Although there was still a clear divide between the staffs, local authority advisers had been working with them for the previous eighteen months and I am sure that this helped to avoid many of the traditional problems of amalgamations. The schools had a joint governing board which had also given a very strong and positive lead, therefore I believed that despite the problems there was an excellent foundation upon which to turn round the fortunes of the new school.

The school began with a raft of measures which were drawn together in an action plan which later became the School Improvement Plan. In the first year most measures concentrated on enabling the school to function as a single organization. The school was in a fortunate financial position as it received a substantial sum of money from Hertfordshire County Council to assist with the amalgamation as well as inheriting a significant underspend from the infants school. The money was spent in an effort to make The Leys Primary School, 'a good place for children to be'. A school motto of 'Friendship and Learning' was devised to promote the fact that we give equal emphasis to social and academic learning. The playgrounds were landscaped and apparatus was installed (they had previously been barren strips of tarmac), and this combined with new supervision arrangements and a new behaviour policy which emphasized positive reinforcement, had an immediate impact on the children's behaviour. A programme of personal and social education was established within the curriculum which included 'circle time' assemblies where children were encouraged to talk about problems, knowing that they would be listened to by everyone. We also reorganized the way the EBD unit worked, and with a new 'teacher in charge' it became a positive asset, both supporting children in mainstream classes and offering a 'time out' facility in return for a properly managed and supported programme of reintegration.

Our school was also the first in Hertfordshire which, in conjunction with our local crime prevention officer, introduced a School Watch scheme. This involved parents and neighbours patrolling the school grounds out of school hours, and keeping a general watch. If any trespassers were spotted, watch members would use their discretion to either ask them to leave or ring the police on a mobile phone which we purchased specially for the scheme. As a result, vandalism has been virtually eliminated, and this has led to a great sense of pride within the local community.

We also took advantage of an opportunity for one of our nursery nurses to train as a leader for a parenting group. This group met on a monthly basis and provided advice and mutual support for parents in addressing common issues encountered when bringing up children. The group was so successful that some of the parents set up their own weekly group at the local community centre where they were able to provide a crèche. We have now combined the sessions and our nursery nurse leads the community centre group once a month.

Gradually, I believe, the school has become the focus which the community lacked — so much that a recent Community Watch survey found that the opportunity to send children to our school was listed as one of the best things about living in the area! We are proud of the progress we have made with the 'friendship' part of our school motto, but it would be wrong to give the impression that anything has been achieved easily, or that anything is perfect. Each of the above paragraphs could be expanded into a chapter of its own, particularly the paragraph on pupil behaviour! Staff still spend a great deal of time and energy supporting emotionally fragile children, but we do not begrudge doing this as we believe that children who find it difficult to behave are entitled to support in the same way that children who find it difficult to read are entitled to support. (Incidentally, we have also been successful in bidding to have a Specific Learning Difficulties Base set up at our school. Although the staff work with children throughout Stevenage and Hitchin, it is very helpful having their expertise so close at hand.)

Gathering data (and acting upon it)

I freely admit that it is only during the last six years that I have become a convert to the need for gathering and analysing the quantity of data that I now

Figure 4.1: Absence rates

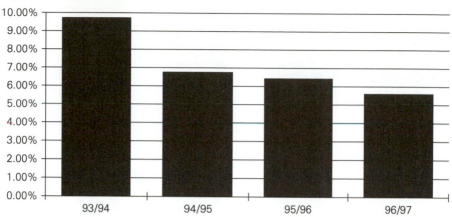

use for assessing the school's performance. When I first received a request from the government to complete a complicated and lengthy return about school attendance rates for the school year 93/94, I was extremely annoyed. However, once completed I was shocked to learn that we had a 9.7 per cent absence rate. This was only just short of the OFSTED indicator for a failing school. The Hertfordshire average was 5.7 per cent and the Stevenage average 6.5 per cent. We set ourselves the target of reducing absence to the Stevenage average.

As the self-esteem of the parent community was so low, I had been following a policy of promoting only good news. Successive news letters talked about the changes and improvements that were being made in the school, and also of course the children's achievements. I did not make any reference to the constant vandalism and other problems we were encountering. I decided that measures to improve attendance must also emphasize the positive.

We began to raise the profile of attendance and punctuality through assemblies, and through the award of half term certificates for all children who achieve 100 per cent attendance. At the end of each term a special large certificate was (and still is) awarded to the class with the best attendance. The importance of regular attendance and punctuality was then the subject of a short paragraph in several news letters. The certificates were highly prized by the children. Suddenly they could gain certificates by simply attending school. Parents began to ring up saying their child was upset because he or she needed a day off school to be treated for head lice (I could write another chapter on head lice!). Did this mean they would lose their certificate? Of course, whenever requested we gave special dispensation. In 1994/95 the absence rate dropped to 6.7 per cent, and has improved for every year since (see Figure 4.1). For the past two years we have been below our target figure!

Raising achievement in the core subjects was more difficult and required more effort. English at Key Stage 1 is a good example. We put in place measures to improve continuity of practice in such things as emergent writing, the

Figure 4.2:   English KS1 teacher assessment — Level 2 and above

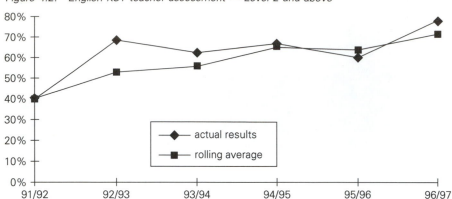

teaching of phonics, etc. Initially we did not set targets, but monitored progress in end of key stage assessments looking at the three-year rolling average to see if we could discern a trend. (The rolling average is based upon an analysis of the combination of three years of results, for example 1994/95, 1995/96 and 1996/97). The rolling average ironed out the peaks and troughs caused by the varying abilities of the various cohorts which can so easily distort perceptions of progress. The focus on literacy appeared to pay dividends with a clear upward trend (see Figure 4.2).

Whereas the setting of targets for improvement for local authorities on a year-by-year basis may be realistic, given the large number of children involved, there is a school of thought that targets related to the three-year rolling average may be more appropriate for individual schools. So far we have not done this, but we did try to take into account the past performance of individual year groups when setting targets for improvement in maths and science for the 96/97 academic year.

Maths is a good example. We knew that our maths teaching needed improvement, but during the first two years of the school's life we had focused on literacy. When we received information about national averages after the first year of KS2 National Curriculum assessments we found that we were close to the national average in English and science, but well below in maths. Therefore, we had done comparatively less well in maths than the other two core subjects and our view of maths teaching was confirmed.

Maths then became the main focus of our school improvement plan. We involved the maths advisory team and looked at resources. Additional resources were purchased which included a set of crude assessments which helped teachers throughout the KS2 part of the school form a view of children's levels of achievement in the different attainment targets. The assessments were conducted early in the spring term so that teachers could use the outcomes in their planning. The assessments also gave teachers an overall view of the abilities of their classes highlighting areas of weakness in the curriculum. As preparation for a forthcoming OFSTED inspection we also asked our link adviser to conduct an OFSTED style inspection focusing on maths. This was extremely helpful, and found that although we had improved our level of resourcing, children were not encountering certain aspects of the curriculum, including place value and data handling, at an early enough stage to be able to achieve Level 4 at the end of KS2.

We set to work to address this, and once again the maths advisory team were helpful letting us have a set of maps for the curriculum which they had been working on even though the maps were only at an early stage of development. Given the changes we had introduced and the ability of the cohort of children, we set ourselves the target of making a 10 per cent improvement in our percentage of children achieving Level 4 at the end of Year 6. In fact we achieved an improvement of 22 per cent! Equally important was the fact that our maths results were no longer out of line with English and science (see Figures 4.3 and 4.4).

Figure 4.3: KS2 maths tests — Level 4 and above*

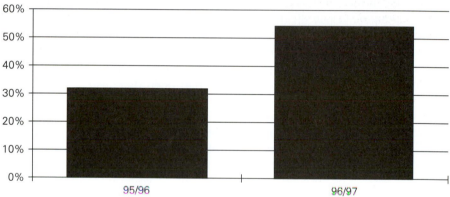

Figure 4.4: 1996–97 KS2 tests — Level 4 and above*

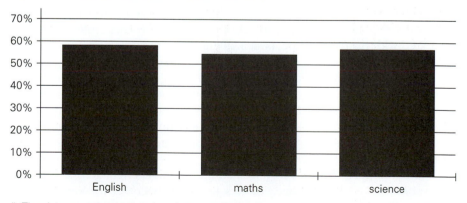

* The data are presented as bar charts as there have not yet been enough years of KS2 tests to produce meaningful three-year rolling averages.

Figure 4.5: KS1 teacher assessment — science Level 2 and above

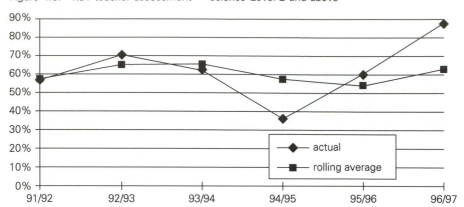

During the same academic year we set targets for improvement in maths and science at KS1. Here we had identified that an increased focus on AT1 in both subjects could pay dividends and again felt that a 10 per cent improvement could be reasonable. In science, staff had found it very difficult to understand the nature of AT1; therefore it had been under-represented in the curriculum, and insufficient opportunity had been given for children to demonstrate achievement. When achievement had been demonstrated, staff had found it difficult to recognize. KS1 staff were supported by the maths and science coordinators.

As can be seen from Figure 4.5 a dramatic 28 per cent improvement in scores year-by-year was achieved, with 88 per cent of children achieving L2 or above. However, we will need to wait for a further year to see if this improvement can be sustained and bring about a significant rise in the three-year rolling average. We are fairly confident that it will, and our target for this year is to match last year's achievement.

This graph also shows the very low results in 94/95 when we first realized that the staff then teaching Year 2 were struggling with science. I blame myself for not picking up on this problem until it was too late. However, when compared with maths in Figure 4.6 it also highlights that this was a very needy year group, and makes the fact that the English results held up that year (we were focusing on English at the time) — a significant achievement which otherwise might have been overlooked! As you can see the year-by-year maths target was achieved with a 12 per cent improvement. This matched our previous best which was in 93/94. We will need to sustain the improvement to raise our three-year rolling average. We are fairly confident we will achieve this, as we did with science.

For our target setting in 96/97 we had not set targets right across the three core subjects at each key stage. Targets had only been set for key areas of focus for the school improvement plan. The targets set had been realistic bearing in mind the prior achievement of the year groups concerned. When

Figure 4.6:   Teacher assessment — maths KS1

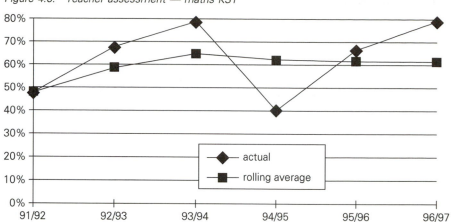

we exceeded the targets we had set ourselves it was a tremendous boost to morale. Staff in Year 2 and Year 6 reported that they had not felt pressurized by the targets, but they were aware of them and they were constantly at the back of their minds. They knew there was an expectation that their children should at least be moving in the direction of the targets, and they knew what they had to do in order to bring about the improvement in achievement that we all thought was possible.

We had made decisions based upon the best information available to us at the time, our knowledge of the children, the way children learn and the curriculum. Improvements were made, and target setting was one element in bringing about that improvement. Vital elements of the process were the short- to medium-term curriculum initiatives in maths and science, but longer term initiatives and structural changes within the school will also have helped. For example, the school has made a substantial commitment to staff development, and has established an ethos where everyone learns from each other. This includes newly qualified teachers as well as teachers a few years away from retirement. Staff generally work and plan together in pairs or in teams which include non-teaching staff who make a very significant contribution. We have also had a deliberate policy of targeting resources at the first three years of schooling, nursery, reception and Year 1. During the autumn term our early years team leader spends 50 per cent of her time supporting the youngest and most needy children in Year 1. She then returns to reception to take in the children who transfer from our nursery in January. This is an expensive policy as it would be possible to not employ a teacher for the autumn term and then to have staff working fixed term contracts for the spring and summer terms. The 96/97 Year 2 cohort were the first to benefit from this investment and therefore some of the improvement could be attributable to it.

Cause and effect is not always easy to decide, however, I believe that target setting has been helpful and for this reason we have extended and formalized our target setting for 97/98.

The future

When the schools first amalgamated to form the new school it was organized into three teams. Early years (nursery, reception, and Y1), Middle school (Years 2, 3 and 4) and Upper school (Years 5 and 6). Each team had a team leader and provided a focus for pastoral support, parent problems, achievement assemblies, etc. and also a focus for curriculum planning. The middle school team acted as a bridge between the two former schools. By September 1997 the bridge was no longer necessary, and I decided to reorganize the school into four teams which were more closely allied to the key stages in the National Curriculum. The teams are now Early years (nursery and reception); Upper infants (Years 1 and 2); Lower juniors (Years 3 and 4) and Upper juniors (Years 5 and 6).

Each team has a clear focus on raising standards in the core subjects within their own two-year period. Targets have been set for improved achievement at the end of each team stage, i.e. reception, Year 2, Year 4 and Year 6. The targets have not been set in the 'comfort zone' but in the 'challenge zone', and are based on the best information we have available about the prior achievement of the year groups.

Year Group	R	2	4	6
Level	1	2	3	4
English	30 (+14)*	80 (+5)	55 (+9)	55 (−4)
Maths	30 (+8)	70 (−8)	55 (+28)	59 (+3)
Science	no target	88 (0)	55 (+19)	54 (−5)

* The numbers in brackets refer to the percentage increase or decrease on the previous year group.

The fact that we have set challenging targets means that inevitably some year groups will not achieve the targets, and exceeding them as we did last year will be extremely difficult. In order that morale is not dented by this it will be important to remember that we may have made significant progress even if the target is not reached. Success needs to be judged by how close we get to the target, and also needs to be judged against the previous achievement of the particular year group. There are some targets where the target figure is lower than the percentage achieved by the previous year group, yet these targets are none the less extremely challenging given the current year group's past record. We will also have to accept that despite our best endeavours we may not get some of our targets right. The targets for the current Year 6 are probably overly ambitious.

The year group has always contained a large number of exceptionally needy children, many of whom have emotional and behavioural problems.

Since Key Stage 1 more needy children have joined the school and able children have left. There are also question marks over the reliability of the teacher assessment in Year 5. However, the staff are aware of what each individual needs to master in order to achieve at a higher level and have not given up hope of achieving the target even though it seems almost certain that we will fall short by between 5 to 10 per cent.

You may be wondering what are we doing differently this year in order to bring about the improvement? Am I just asking staff to work harder to raise standards? Early years is benefiting from a change in admissions policy which brings children into reception in September and January, instead of September, January and April as was previously the case. We have also been a pilot school for the National Literacy Project (NLP) which we have introduced in Reception, Year 1 and Year 2. (We are beginning the introduction of NLP in KS2 during the summer term.) Upper infants are consolidating their work in maths and science as well as benefiting from NLP. (We are very enthusiastic about NLP.) Science at KS2 has been a focus for the school, with the science coordinator leading in service training, and we have also introduced target setting at an individual child level, although I would say that both these initiatives are probably at too early a stage to have a significant impact in the lower junior team. In the Upper junior team our maths teaching has developed into a team teaching approach involving setting across Years 5 and 6, we have had a major focus on writing which has involved all the children setting their own personal targets for improvement, and over Easter the children in Year 6 are having a 'sponsored science fact learning challenge'. Any money raised will go towards a leavers party! Perhaps not the most educationally inspiring idea but the children have certainly warmed to it.

Although all our targets are threshold targets, i.e. L2 and above at KS1, L4 and above at KS2. Staff are keenly aware of the progress of children who are not around that threshold level, for example, children in Year 6 for whom achieving Level 3 or Levels 5 or 6 would be a challenge. For this reason in future years we may set our targets based upon an average points score which would reflect the achievement of all our children. Using more than one measure to judge progress is an interesting exercise anyway and can give surprising results. When we were preparing for our OFSTED inspection, I did some work looking at the point score improvement of our 95/96 Year 6. This was the year group which had had such low results at the end of KS1 prior to the amalgamation. As luck would have it theirs were the most recent results that the inspectors would have to go on. I used point scores as opposed to the number of children at Level 4 and above, as this was the method used by OFSTED when compiling their statistical report for the inspection team. I was both surprised and pleased by the results.

As can be seen in Figure 4.7, even though our children scored below the national average on threshold levels, we exceeded national averages on points score. This is because we had more children at Levels 5 and 6 than the national average. The graph also shows that our children had made well above national

Figure 4.7:   Point score improvement Y6 — 95/96

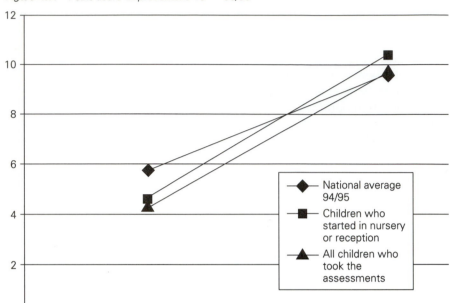

average progress, and, not surprisingly, those who had had a settled education made the best progress.

Conclusion

Many colleagues are struggling with the necessity of setting targets for the first time across the three core subjects (five if you include ICT (Information and Communications Technology) and RE) and our school is no different, as in the past we have set targets focused on specific areas for improvement. What I have tried to show is that target setting cannot be divorced from the process of school improvement, and that the most difficult question is not how to set the targets but how to bring about the improvement. Targets provide a focus for school improvement activity and at my school have certainly been borne in mind by the staff concerned. The targets have not produced unreasonable pressure as they have been linked to specific initiatives. They were set using the best available data to compare achievements between subjects, to compare our own school's performance against national data, and to make realistic predictions for individual cohorts of children.

I am conscious that the period of time we have taken may appear somewhat luxurious given the current pressures to make rapid improvement. However, I make no apologies for this as we all know that making significant, sound, sustainable educational progress is, in athletics terms, more like being a long distance runner than a sprinter! I am also conscious of the fact that we have made and are making mistakes — for example, the overambitious targets for Year 6. We have always discussed the available data on the children's achievements with governors, and for the past two years we have published our targets in our School Improvement Plan. A copy of this plan goes to every governor and member of staff, teaching and non-teaching. However, this is very different from publishing our targets to parents in general. Clearly, once again there will be potential for schools to be unfairly portrayed in a negative light. Despite what may appear in the local press, the most important audience for schools is their own parent community, and parents are usually much better informed, and far more sympathetic, about their own children's school than they are about the perceived state of education nationally. It is up to us to make sure that our parents get accurate information, and a realistic interpretation of that information. We intend to be proactive, therefore I do not think that the wider publication of targets will be a problem for us, and you may rest assured that any improvements will be celebrated whether the targets are hit or not!

Finally, I have tried to show that, as well as schools having a clear focus on raising standards in the core subjects, it is important that they are good places for children to be. Success in this respect cannot be divorced from working closely with parents and the local community. It requires a broad curriculum that includes personal and social education and many other things that there has not been space to touch upon in this chapter, such as the creative arts. It also requires the commitment of a very large number of people, both employed and voluntary. We have had that commitment at The Leys and for that, on behalf of the children, I am very grateful.

5 The Role of the LEA in Supporting Assessment in the Primary School

Sue Swaffield

Introduction

Teachers in primary schools have always assessed pupils' performance, and continue to do so as an integral part of their everyday teaching. In 1988 the introduction of statutory assessment requirements into the primary phase, with national tests and tasks and summative teacher assessment, focused on 7- and 11-year-olds. The role of the Local Education Authority (LEA) in supporting schools with both ongoing and statutory assessment has been determined largely by two parallel and interrelating strands of development.

First, the National Curriculum and its assessment arrangements. These have been determined centrally, and have undergone a number of changes and revisions since their introduction through the Education Reform Act in 1988. Second, LEA structures and ways of working with schools. These have been influenced by decisions taken centrally, such as the increasing devolution of funding to schools. However, requirements have been responded to in different ways locally, so that some LEAs maintained a very centralized and proactive role, whereas others, sometimes geographically adjacent, reduced their work with schools to the minimum statutorily required. Riley and Rowles (Townsend, 1997) categorize LEAs in respect of their approaches in working with schools, identifying a continuum ranging from interventionist, interactive and responsive, through to non-interventionist. These categories are not necessarily discrete nor exclusive: an LEA may be broadly interventionist in some respects, and responsive in others. Also, the particular approaches taken by an LEA are likely to change over time.

In May 1997 there was a change of government, when the Conservative Party, which had been in office for eighteen years was replaced by a Labour government with a large majority. Although the Labour government carried on with many of the education policies of the Conservatives, the role of the LEAs altered considerably, often in ways directly related to assessment.

This chapter traces the changing role of the LEA in supporting schools with assessment, it is divided into three parts and includes an illustrative case study. The first section examines the period from the introduction of the National Curriculum and its assessment arrangements in 1988 until the change of government in 1997. The second section looks at the position immediately following the general election, while the final section looks into the future and discusses the role that LEAs might and should fulfil. The case study, situated chronologically between the second and third sections, looks at the interplay in relation to assessment between one particular school and its LEA.

Past

National Curriculum assessment arrangements were informed by the Task Group on Assessment and Testing (TGAT) chaired by Professor Paul Black, which presented its main report to Kenneth Baker, then Secretary of State for Education, on December 24, 1987 (DES, 1987). The main report set out a rationale and structure for National Curriculum assessment, and the group presented three supplementary reports in March of the following year. The third supplementary report was *A System of Support*, recommending national agencies, regional tiers and district groups to provide a comprehensive system of implementation, administration and support. The report proposed a programme consisting of awareness raising for headteachers, training for teachers in continuous assessment and the administration of tests and tasks, and moderation activities.

The proposals of TGAT's third supplementary report were not fully implemented. In particular, regional structures were not established. TGAT anticipated this by detailing some of the difficulties that might arise in the absence of established regional structures, and predicting the scope for *ad hoc* structures. The formation of the Association of Assessment Inspectors and Advisers, with its regional groups, constitutional requirement for moderation and majority LEA personnel membership, was one such response.

TGAT's main report envisaged that LEAs would have a major part to play in implementing the proposals. The three principal roles for LEAs that TGAT identified were: training for teachers in the requisite knowledge, understanding and skills; arrangements for moderation; and the provision and publication of information.

The School Examinations and Assessment Council [SEAC] identified five principal functions for LEAs in relation to assessment (SEAC, 1993):

- support for schools (e.g. documents, guidance, moderation, cluster work, work with parents and governors);
- training for the professional development of teachers and other staff;
- recruitment and employment of staff (e.g. for training and moderation);
- administrative support for schools;
- evaluations.

The National Curriculum was introduced progressively from the autumn of 1989, and so LEAs' support for schools was dovetailed into this timetable, with the initial focus in primary schools on Key Stage 1 (children aged 5–7 years). The phasing in of the National Curriculum and the directing of associated funding for training at Key Stage 1 and Key Stage 3 (children aged 11–14 years), meant that Key Stage 2 (children aged 7–11 years) was marginalized. The problem was exacerbated for junior (Key Stage 2 only) schools, because unless special provision was made by the LEA they did not even have easy access to the assessment materials. LEAs targeted the recipients of training, often concentrating on headteachers and possibly deputies first, closely followed by Year 2 teachers, and later other teachers in Key Stage 1.

One of the first tasks for LEAs was to explain the structure and vocabulary of the National Curriculum and its assessment. Another was to emphasize the importance of the programmes of study, detailing what had to be taught, rather than the criteria for assessment. This remained an uphill struggle, though, with the assessment arrangements continuing to take precedence over the programmes of study right through until the revision of the Curriculum in 1995.

The National Curriculum as originally introduced had 14 areas of attainment in mathematics, and 17 in science. Orders were laid before Parliament at the end of 1991 to reduce these to five and four respectively. Teachers had to relearn the attainment targets, to know how the old ones had become subsumed into the new ones, and to revise their recording systems accordingly. LEA advisers provided corresponding maps and other documentation to assist teachers in this transition.

In 1993 there was a major review of the National Curriculum and its assessment, led by Sir Ron Dearing. The subsequent revision required teachers to move away from using statements of attainment and a set formula (such as, the child must achieve all, or all but one of them listed for a particular level) for arriving at end of key stage teacher assessments, to using level descriptions (a broad statement about characteristics of performance) and an all round judgment. This required teachers to get to know the level descriptions, to understand how to use them, and to redesign their records so as to provide supportive information. Once again, schools and teachers looked to the LEAs for guidance. The extent to which it was provided largely depended upon the structure and ethos of the LEA at the time.

Skills and techniques generally take much longer to acquire than knowledge, and require a different approach. Training approaches included advisers working alongside teachers in class, and very commonly, agreement trialling sessions, often with clusters of schools. The role of LEA staff, whether they were advisers, advisory teachers, or seconded teachers, was to offer practical ideas and suggestions, and to manage agreement trialling sessions. In so doing, they also provided a model for teachers to follow when working with colleagues in their own schools. Given the scale of the training required and the limits on funding, it was often necessary to employ a cascade model, although as Lee (1993) reports, this was often not well received. The attendee felt pressurized to disseminate, and the other teachers felt that they were missing out. Therefore, the LEA trainers also had to support the teachers attending sessions to fulfil their role as disseminators.

Some LEAs produced training materials, for example in the form of videos, to develop teachers' skills such as observation and the associated classroom management techniques. Another way in which LEAs supported schools was by the provision of documentation, particularly policy guidelines, and recording and reporting formats. Initially most LEAs were fairly prescriptive, but as LEAs themselves became more disparate, the amount and strength of guidance became more varied.

The effect of the early concentration upon Key Stage 1 began to be picked up through inspections which revealed that assessment practice in Key Stage 2 was lagging behind that in Key Stage 1 (OFSTED, 1996). Central government responded to this by announcing a new category of Grant for Education Support and Training for 1996/7 aimed at enhancing teacher's assessment skills in Key Stage 2. The timing of this announcement meant that some LEAs found themselves unable to provide the required matched funding and did not take up the grant. Those that did responded in a variety of ways, for example by providing half-day courses for all Year 6 teachers; running five-day accredited courses for teachers from any year in Key Stage 2; or devolving the funding completely to schools. This training opportunity for Key Stage 2 continued in the GEST allocations for 1997/8 and the Standards Fund for 1998/9.

From the introduction of the National Curriculum assessment arrangements, LEAs have been involved in one way or another with Key Stage 1 audit. The precise requirements have changed over time; initially LEAs were required to ensure the satisfactory administration of tasks and tests, as well as the accuracy of teacher assessment judgments. Teachers filled cupboards with children's work to provide the required evidence. Later the responsibility for teacher assessment judgments was dropped (although a legacy remains in some teachers being wedded to keeping vast amounts of children's work 'because someone might ask for it'), and from 1998 the requirement on LEAs is to audit a sample of Key Stage 1 schools, rather than all of them.

In 1993 SEAC indicated that 'the principal role of the LEA is to act as auditor of assessment standards' (SEAC, 1993). In those LEAs where funding and strategic decisions led to a paring down of the LEA role to the statutory minimum, this did indeed become the case. Other LEAs were able to continue to provide considerable professional support and advice.

In order for all children to have the opportunity to demonstrate their attainment through National Curriculum assessment, provision can be made to meet individual needs. For example, some children may have specific difficulties which significantly affect the speed of their reading or writing and require additional time for the tests. LEAs have been required to consider, and where appropriate grant, schools' requests for special arrangements for the Key Stage 2 and 3 tests.

LEAs were, and continue to be, responsible for collecting Key Stage 1 results. The relationship that LEAs began building with schools at this time about the collection, holding and use of performance data, has had far-reaching effects. A few have been able to combine this established trust with a proactive role and have built up detailed and robust databases. Most, however, felt themselves progressively sidelined, as results from Key Stages 2 and 3 were collected by external agencies. This trend was not reversed until the change of government in 1997, when LEAs became responsible for publishing end of Key Stage 2 assessment information, and were encouraged to take a greater lead in the management and use of assessment data.

Quite a number of LEAs worked with their schools on developing forms of baseline assessment. As this was not initially a statutory requirement, practice between LEAs often varied considerably, and again reflected the differing stances that the LEAs took in relation to their role and responsibilities.

Although TGAT had emphasized four purposes of assessment, including diagnostic and formative, the statutory requirements and huge array of practical requirements meant that much of the early work concentrated on assessment *of* learning, particularly through end of key stage assessment arrangements, rather than assessment *for* learning. Nevertheless, LEAs have always supported the notion that assessment by teachers is an integral part of teaching and learning, and provides much valuable information that can and should be used to enhance teaching and learning. This has been demonstrated through the documentation provided by LEAs, including policies and guidance advocating constructive marking and feedback to children and the involvement of the children in the assessment process, and through messages given at training sessions.

Present

The LEA's recent and present role in supporting schools consists of the continuation of some established elements and others more recently introduced. These are partly a result of the change of government in May 1997, although many of the changes had been planned by the previous administration and implemented by the new one.

Many schools still welcome training sessions provided by their LEA alerting them to the often subtle but significant changes in the statutory assessment arrangements and requirements. Baseline assessment moves from being optional to statutory as from September 1998, with LEAs needing to ensure that they have an accredited scheme (whether being of their own devising or one adopted from elsewhere). There are training implications, as well as monitoring, data collection and analysis.

As the LEA's statutory role in relation to audit of Key Stage 1 is reduced to auditing a sample of schools each year rather than them all, LEAs are looking to provide the support for consistency of teachers' assessments in other ways. For example, the encouragement of agreement trialling in clusters of schools.

An increasing emphasis from central government is on the security arrangements connected with end of key stage tests, and measures to eliminate any suspicion of malpractice. LEAs' role in monitoring the administrative arrangements is being extended from Key Stage 1 to include Key Stages 2 and 3, where LEA officials (inspectors or advisers) are expected to carry out spot checks in a sample of schools before, during and immediately after the test period. The consideration of requests for special arrangements for tests, and the monitoring of these arrangements, continues to be a function of the LEA.

The role of the LEA in relation to the collection, checking, analysis and publication of assessment data has increased. More data are becoming available, for example, through the introduction of baseline assessment. LEAs are being given functions which were previously carried out by other agencies, specifically in relation to Key Stage 2. Primary school performance tables were originally published by the DfEE, but the results from 1997 and subsequent years are published locally.

There is more and more emphasis on the use that can be made of assessment data, for example to provide benchmark information, to inform target setting, and to enable value added calculations. The white paper *Excellence in Schools* (DfEE, 1997a), in discussing National Curriculum assessment data says: 'We must put all the available information to work' (25).

One way of putting the data to work is the setting of school targets, which are a requirement from September 1998, but which many schools, with advice from their LEAs, began before this date. The LEA's role in target setting is:

- to provide schools with data and guidance to help them set targets;
- to challenge, where necessary, draft targets set by the schools, ensuring that they are appropriately demanding, and that when taken collectively will enable the LEA to meet the target set for it by government for 2002;
- to help schools meet their targets;
- to monitor the schools' performance.

The National Literacy Project was initiated by the Conservative government and carried forward by the Labour government. With its aim and monitoring being based on national, LEA and school levels of performance at the end of Key Stage 2 in National Curriculum English tests, assessment obviously has a vital role.

Another initiative whose effectiveness is judged largely by the assessment of children's learning is the summer schools for low attaining readers. Introduced for the first time in the summer of 1997, claims of their effectiveness were based on the assessment of reading ages (DfEE, 1997b). All of these activities relate predominantly to assessment *of* learning.

Data, at the level of individual pupils and marks on test questions, can also be used diagnostically, emphasizing assessment *for* learning. Various pieces of commercially produced software exist to assist this process, and LEAs can recommend and support specific software.

The use of data on transfer has typically been a rather neglected aspect of schools' practice, and LEAs have been varied in the lead that they have given to schools. However, a number of factors have made this an important focus for all LEAs. Two publications (SCAA, 1996; 1997) promote progression through the use of data, especially between primary and secondary schools. In 1998/9 a Standards Fund category was created by central government specifically to support schools in making maximum use of National Curriculum information available from the previous key stage. In addition, the help provided by the LEA to ensure successful transition of pupils through the phases of education is one of the proposed criteria for judgment in the inspection of local authorities. LEA support for schools in the use of data on transfer falls into two main categories: mechanistic and professional. As more and more individual pupil assessment data (baseline, end of key stage test, task and teacher assessment results, optional information such as age standardized results, Year 4 test results and other test results) becomes available, so it becomes increasingly necessary for these data to be transferred electronically. It is the LEA which is in a position to lead and coordinate. Having information is one thing, using it is another, and it is here that the LEA's professional development role comes in. Secondary colleagues tend to use data only when they have confidence in them. This confidence comes with understanding, which is enhanced by cross phase working. Many schools work in various ways with their feeder schools, and LEAs can support these practices where they exist and encourage them where they do not exist.

The revised OFSTED framework requires inspectors to judge the extent to which teachers assess pupils' work thoroughly and constructively and use assessments to inform teaching. Analysis of inspection reports identifies trends and weaknesses. This has alerted LEAs to the need to help schools address issues arising, such as using assessment information to inform planning and teaching; to use a wider repertoire of assessment techniques; to employ consistent and constructive marking policies; and to involve pupils. LEAs' training programmes reflect these points and help contribute to teachers' understanding of assessment *for* learning. By emphasizing the role of assessment for learning, LEAs are helping schools to meet their own, and thus the LEAs', targets.

An important role that LEAs play in school improvement, including those aspects related to assessment, is putting schools in touch with others from whom to learn. No school is a 'good' school in all respects, and the LEA's knowledge of practice and strengths of individual schools can be used to make very powerful and constructive links. In order to illustrate the ways in which LEAs have worked with schools, the next section provides an example with reference to one primary school.

The LEA and the school: An illustrative case study

The purpose of this case study is to show how assessment in one school has been supported by the LEA. It does this by tracing the development of assessment practice and policy in the school and relating it to the role of the LEA. A model for analysing the different ways schools are supported is also discussed.

Buckden School is a large primary school serving two villages, although about half of its 400 children come from beyond this catchment area. The school is organized into four units of similarly aged children, which engenders a very strong team ethic among the teachers, who review and plan together. The unit leaders, key stage coordinator and deputy head all have significant roles within the school, and there is a history of staff moving on from these positions to headships and deputy headships elsewhere. This culture presents a challenge to the school, in the extent to which new staff understand, agree and implement policies.

Buckden is within Cambridgeshire, an LEA serving nearly 300 educational establishments. In the early 1990s the LEA's support for schools moved along the continuum identified by Riley and Rowles (Townsend, 1997) towards the responsive and non-interventionist. Before 1990, advisers and advisory teachers operating from 16 separate centres were centrally funded and provided courses and in-school support, but there was little attempt at curriculum coordination or coverage. Teams of curriculum support teachers were then established, covering the phases of schooling and the geographical areas of the county, and a market aspect was introduced. Further restructuring followed, characterized by a high level of devolution of inservice funding to schools, the establishment of an agency for advisory work operating as a quasi-business, and drastically reduced numbers of advisers. In 1997 a new advisory service, including additional advisers ensuring curriculum coverage and greater central funding became operational. These changes are in line with the trend identified by Riley and Rowles of LEAs moving back along the continuum towards greater pro-activity, although there is some negotiation about the nature and level of intervention. Throughout these changes the advisory and inspectorate functions of the LEA have remained separate but related.

Harland (1990) identified four modes in which advisory teachers worked with classroom teachers. These can be described as giving, telling, showing and asking. Relating these to the current mantra of 'pressure and support' and more broadly to the role of the LEA through a variety of personnel, it can be seen that the first three together constitute support whereas the asking mode reflects the pressure or challenge.

Assessment practice at Buckden has evolved in line with national developments and is documented in its assessment policies. The early stages of implementing National Curriculum assessment were supported by the LEA through training sessions for headteachers and deputies, which tended to concentrate on the telling mode of operation. The school's assessment policy drawn up during this period had as its aims:

- using assessment to ensure that the curriculum matches the needs of all children;
- enabling the teacher to decide how the learning should be taken forward;
- providing evidence of achievement, to be used evaluatively, and to give information to others.

The procedures detailed in the 1991 policy concentrate very much on the concerns of the time — how to ensure that all aspects of English, mathematics and science were assessed for all children, and the collection and retention of evidence. The use of assessment as an indicator for further work was also addressed, by giving teachers examples of strategies that may be needed to develop further understanding, as well as considering the classroom organization which supports good assessment practice.

The following year a policy on records of achievement was adopted. The development of this practice in school built on attendance by the assessment coordinator at a series of sessions run by the LEA on 'Primary Records of Achievement'. These sessions looked at the underpinning purposes and principles of records of achievement, gave opportunities for discussion and reflection on involving children in their learning, and provided examples. To use Harland's categorization, there was a mixture of telling, asking and giving.

Buckden's assessment policy was revised in 1993, to include the assessment and recording of aspects of English and mathematics at the beginning and the end of the year, as well as at the end of blocks of work as previously; more detail on planning for assessment; and making use of past statutory assessment materials.

The revision of the National Curriculum and its assessment arrangements, heralded by the Dearing reports (NCC and SEAC, 1993; SCAA, 1993), necessitated another review of assessment practice and policy within the school. The headteacher negotiated in-school support for this process from the LEA, where an adviser worked over a period of time variously with the headteacher, the assessment coordinator, unit leaders, and the whole staff. Although working with the headteacher, the assessment coordinator and unit leaders in examining current practice and policy and planning future developments, the adviser's role was one of critical friend, but the whole staff sessions tended to be more instructive — in other words, a combination of asking and telling. One outcome of this work was a 1995 assessment policy, reflecting changes in practice. Particularly significant developments were the detailed planning for assessment being followed through from termly plans to weekly and daily plans; the instigation of a school portfolio (a collection of assessed work which demonstrates teachers' understanding of the National Curriculum levels, and which supports teachers in their future judgment making); a new format for recording assessments against learning objectives, rather than 'statements of attainment' which were no longer in the revised Curriculum; and annual teacher assessments against the National Curriculum levels.

An OFSTED inspection in 1996 commended the assessment practice at the school, and gave Buckden the impetus to consider how teaching was taking place, rather than concentrating on what was being taught. In assessment terms, this was done through reviewing and revising the records of achievement, linked with the sharing of clear learning objectives and individual target setting. An adviser again worked with the staff over a number of sessions, leading activities, which necessitated the staff reflecting on their practice and prompting them to plan developments. The balance was very much on the asking mode, with some telling. It is the critical questioning as a prompt to review, and development, which the headteacher values and seeks from the LEA.

Following this period of inservice training, one way in which sharing learning objectives with children has been kept alive as an issue has been to make it a focus for teacher appraisal. This has also provided the mechanism for support for teachers.

Statutory assessment arrangements at the school continue to be supported by the LEA through the provision of courses and audit arrangements. The school's assessment data are put in context locally and nationally by the LEA's statistician and research officer. Benchmarking information, enabling the school to compare its performance with other similar schools, is also provided for the school by the LEA. These instances of 'giving' by the LEA are closely followed, in the process of target setting, by 'asking', where an LEA inspector discusses the targets set by the school to ensure that they are appropriately challenging, before agreeing them.

The headteacher sees the priorities for assessment in the school in terms of consolidating practice, especially with staff changes, and continually emphasizing the importance of formative assessment and the involvement of children in the process, particularly within the context of proliferating standardized tests nationally. The headteacher describes assessment as being one of the cornerstones of the school, and a necessary and integral part of the curriculum.

Future

Barbara Lee, writing in 1993 (Lee, 1993), reported that teachers felt that the pressures to sort out their immediate needs in relation to assessment were so great that they could not afford to spend time reflecting on underlying principles. Lee expressed the hope that once assessment and recording procedures had become familiar and more routine, teachers, guided by their LEAs, would consider some of the broader issues. This was not presented as a hope for the far distant future; Lee suggested that the work could be carried out in the context of the preparation of school development plans, for which GEST funding was available in 1993/4. Several years later it appears that teachers have continued to have to deal with immediate demands arising as a result of continued change, for example, the revised curriculum and assessment arrangements. So the need for teachers to reflect on underlying principles remains. This is not to say that there is no understanding of the issues, but rather that it is not widespread. LEAs routinely apply and refer to principles of assessment during training, but understandably teachers under pressure tend to want the 'how' rather than the 'why'.

In the initial stages of target setting, the emphasis is on using data to set appropriate targets. However, actually setting the target is only the beginning.

LEAs, schools and teachers need to take action to achieve the targets, and to maintain improvement over time. The difficulty that schools encounter in maintaining improvement rates beyond three or four years have been studied by Professor John Gray. He found that schools have not concentrated on achieving substantial improvements in the quality of teaching and learning (unpublished survey reported in the *Times Educational Supplement* 28.11.97). A paper by Paul Black and Dylan Wiliam, in 'Assessment and classroom learning' (Black and Wiliam, 1998) states that formative assessment does improve learning, and that gains in achievement appear to be quite considerable. It seems that it will be both imperative and fruitful for LEAs to reemphasize the role of assessment *for* learning. This will not be a quick or easy fix, though. Black talks of a set of guiding principles, rather than any optimum model, which underpin the fundamental changes needed in every classroom. Thus LEAs will need to guide teachers in the exploration and understanding of these principles, so that teachers can develop new skills and change their classroom practice. Neither understanding nor skills can be developed easily or quickly, and so there is a very major role for LEAs in their work with schools.

Another approach, which it is claimed, has significant effects on pupils' learning, is that of accelerated learning; other techniques take into account recent research into the functioning of the brain and pupils' different learning styles. If teachers, headteachers, parents, governors, the LEA itself, OFSTED and central government are to be persuaded of the efficacy of such methods, there may well need to be some research where the effect of these approaches can be demonstrated. In this case, evidence of improvement through the comparisons of assessment *of* learning before and after the employment of these methods may be required. It is at the LEA level that such research could be initiated and monitored.

The statutory requirements for assessment and target setting concentrate on the core subjects of English, mathematics and science. There is some justifiable concern that this leads to a narrowing of the curriculum, and a devaluing of aspects such as personal and social education. Although many recognize the importance of these aspects in themselves and as a necessary prerequisite for all effective learning, researchers are beginning to explore ways of making children's learning in these areas more explicit and quantifiable. The expansion of this work is considered by some to be a very important focus for development. Individual LEAs may pursue certain lines, while networking between LEAs enables them to support their schools more fully. The assessment of learning beyond the core should achieve much greater prominence and expertise in the future.

The assessment of children working at very low levels is an area which concerns many professionals and which would benefit from development. Many children with special needs will never attain a Level 1 in any aspect of the National Curriculum, but they are still learning and making progress. Some LEAs have already produced materials to support schools in the teaching and assessment of children at this level (for example, Manchester Inspection and

Advisory Service, 1997) but there is scope for much more work identifying the small steps of progress.

The consideration of the important interplay of ethics, equity and assessment is not new (see Gipps, 1990), but is an area which does not seem to have been addressed very thoroughly at the school level. LEAs must have a role here in the future. It is perhaps another example of the need identified by Lee for teachers to reflect upon principles. Issues of ethics and assessment arise, for example, in 'teaching to the test'. Gipps (1994) sets out instances where this would be seen as unethical, and describes situations where it would be professionally acceptable. Teachers need to understand and debate the principles and subtleties involved if they are to reconcile and develop a clear view of some of the conflicting pressures they often feel about their practice in preparing children for statutory assessment. This debate should be led by the LEA. Equity and assessment concerns the extent to which the assessment procedures enable all children to demonstrate their learning. At the everyday level this is within teachers' sphere of influence. Teachers are used to the idea of differentiation in order for different children to learn different things in different ways, but perhaps are less aware and skilled in enabling different children to show what they have learnt in different ways. This concept has been developed by Butler, among others, in her work on style (Butler, 1995). This is another area of assessment practice where LEAs should take a lead.

Lifelong learning is an aspiration of past and present governments but one which has still got a long way to go. One aspect of development in this area is the revision of the National Record of Achievement and the processes and materials that support it. Since lifelong learning and the National Record of Achievement (or whatever it may be called in the future) is for all, teachers are included. A few LEAs have encouraged primary school teachers to engage in the process of reviewing, recording and planning their achievements and experiences, but this is an area with the potential for much greater activity.

All the points discussed in this section relate to new or previously rather ignored aspects of the LEAs work in supporting schools with assessment. Alongside these, many functions which are already in place and have been examined in previous sections will need to continue.

Conclusion

Although LEAs have undoubtedly played a very influential role in supporting schools with assessment, it should be remembered that LEAs are not the only bodies which can and do fulfil this function. The decline of LEAs in the early and mid-1990s saw a corresponding rise in private companies and individuals offering support to schools. In many cases the personnel were originally employed by LEAs.

Since the introduction of the National Curriculum and its assessment arrangements, LEAs have had a continuously developing role in supporting schools. Their ability and central government's expectation that they do this has changed over time — starting off as being quite central, diminishing as the Conservative administration went on, and then being resurrected with the change of government in 1997. However, 1997 saw not only a greater role for LEAs in supporting schools, but also much greater expectations and accountabilities. LEAs are themselves to be inspected, and any LEA that is found not to be supporting its schools adequately can expect to find its powers removed.

Whoever provides support to schools on assessment, the emphasis has been very much upon the assessment *of* learning. An awareness of how individual children and schools are performing undoubtedly focuses attention on improving standards. However, long term and continued improvement will only be achieved by a much greater use of assessment *for* learning. This is an aspect that has received comparatively very little attention as yet, and one which LEAs, with their holistic relationship with schools and teachers, are in a good position to develop.

References

BLACK, P. and WILIAM, D. (1998) 'Assessment and classroom learning', *Assessment in Education* **5**, (1).

BUTLER, K. (1995) *Viewpoints*, Columbia Conn: The Learner's Dimension.

DfEE (1997a) *Excellence in Schools*, London: DfEE.

DfEE (1997b) *The Summer Literary Schools: An Evaluation of the 1997 Pilot Scheme by Education Extra*, London: DfEE.

DES (1987) *National Curriculum: Task Group on Assessment and Testing*, London: HMSO.

GIPPS, C. (1990) *Assessment: A Teachers' Guide to the Issues*, London: Hodder and Stoughton.

GIPPS, C. (1994) *Beyond Testing*, London: Falmer Press.

HARLAND, J. (1990) *The Work and Impact of Advisory Teachers*, Slough: NFER.

LEE, B. (1993) *Supporting Assessment in Schools: The Role of the LEA*, Slough: NFER.

MANCHESTER INSPECTION AND ADVISORY SERVICE (1997) *Standards for Assessing Progress in Communication/Speaking and Listening Pre-Level 1 of the National Curriculum*, Manchester: City Council Education Department.

NCC AND SEAC (1993) *The National Curriculum and its Assessment: Interim Report*, York NCC and London SEAC.

OFSTED (1996) *Subjects and Standards: Issues for School Development Arising from OFSTED Inspection Findings 1994–5, Key Stages 1 and 2*, London: HMSO.

SCAA (1993) *The National Curriculum and its Assessment: Final Report*, London: SCAA.

SCAA (1996) *Promoting Continuity between Key Stage 2 and Key Stage 3*, London: SCAA.

SCAA (1997) *Making Effective Use of Key Stage 2 Assessments*, London: SCAA.

SEAC (1993) *School Assessment Folder 1993*, London: SEAC.

TOWNSEND, T. (ed.) (1997) *Restructuring and Quality*, London: Routledge.

6 Baseline Assessment: Policy into Practice

Sally Threlfall and Jenny Woodbridge

Introduction

From September 1998 it will be a statutory requirement for all maintained primary schools in England to use an accredited baseline scheme with all children starting their reception year. The scheme must be capable of producing numerical outcomes related to a specific range of achievements. Debate has focused on both the appropriateness and usefulness of viewing young children's learning from this perspective.

This chapter aims to inform this debate by setting baseline assessment within an approach developed by Leeds Education Authority (LEA) which:

- has the best interest of children at heart;
- is rooted within a set of accepted early years principles (The principles underpinning the scheme described in this chapter are included as an appendix);
- is consistent with what is widely recognized as evolving effective practice in early years assessment.

In focusing on key questions that staff within the Advisory and Inspection Service and schools faced as they developed and implemented the authority-wide baseline assessment scheme, *A Framework for Entry Assessment* (Leeds Education, 1997), implications for practice will be highlighted. The need to embed baseline assessment within a process of qualitative assessment practice is a consistent theme. The chapter concludes by raising questions that require continual debate if the purposes of baseline assessment are to be achieved and the learning experiences of children enriched.

Why do we need baseline assessment?

To ensure effective planning of the curriculum, the assessment of children when they enter reception classes has been carried out for many years. However, during the last few years, the political prominence given to school performance and accountability and the need to set children's progress at the end of Key Stage 1, within the context of their on-entry performance, has made quantitative baseline assessment inevitable. These two differing notions are identified as key purposes in *The National Framework for Baseline Assessment* (SCAA, 1997):

- to provide information to help teachers plan effectively to meet children's individual learning needs;
- to measure children's attainment, using one or more numerical outcomes which can be used in later value-added analysis of children's progress.

Although consensus regarding the first purpose is assured, since it underpins effective teaching and learning, the second purpose is more contentious as it has the potential for imposing a curriculum and mode of teaching that will not truly reflect early years principles.

How did the Leeds *Framework for Entry Assessment* evolve?

A strong commitment to early years is an established feature of the Advisory Service within the (LEA). In September 1994 a plan was established to support the development of a framework that would stimulate high quality entry assessment practices, based on a sound knowledge and understanding of young learners, underpinned by secure principles and rooted within qualitative assessment practice. The plan aimed to stimulate a process where practitioners would challenge their existing practice in the spirit of critical enquiry and self-evaluation.

The developmental process began with a city-wide conference addressed by Mary Jane Drummond. The tone and message was upbeat and successful in raising awareness and setting the scene for change. A detailed and comprehensive programme of courses followed up the issues raised. The courses sought to develop good assessment practice and were at no time delivering a prescribed recipe for change. The process aimed to develop a framework that would support practitioners seeking to improve their practice.

Working parties of committed practitioners were set up to develop materials and identify the scope of current good practice and future development. Each group worked autonomously and independently to a particular brief. A powerful and positive consensus emerged from each of the six working groups. The framework for entry assessment had three clear qualitative stages: the initial contacts made; the qualitative profiles and records kept; and the summative reports written. Through each of these stages ran two common threads: observation and the partnership with parents.

The working parties had considered only qualitative issues, and the materials generated formed the basis of the written framework. Quantifiable baseline assessment became the fourth stage in the process of entry assessment, and it was devised by the early years team within the Advisory and Inspection Service.

How can quantitative and qualitative assessment be effectively linked?

The reasons why the conference, courses and working parties had only addressed qualitative issues were rooted in the clear knowledge and understanding of young learners of all participants. It takes a long time for young children to share their achievements and testing measures often result in underestimation. Observation-led assessment, in a variety of contexts over time, represents the most appropriate and effective method of assessment in the early years. However, the imperative on the national agenda was for quantitative measures to provide hard evidence to support the standards and school improvement debate. This national pressure was supported locally by senior officers within the authority and managers in school.

This presented the early years team with a dilemma. An ambivalence towards quantifying the on-entry achievement of young learners had to be set against the reality of the fast approaching statutory requirement. There was a need to compromise with the realities of the situation, but not with the underpinning early years principles. The challenge was to find ways of quantifying evidence gained through good qualitative practice. The result was baseline descriptions of entry achievement for language, mathematics and social and emotional development on a five-point scale.

The baseline descriptions for language and mathematics were written for each of the strands of the National Curriculum. This was done to facilitate comparative analysis with later standardized assessments. The descriptions sought to integrate appropriate achievements and competencies with what young learners might do to demonstrate that achievement. Baseline judgments would be made by best fit analysis using observable evidence of achievement. Examples from the scales are included in Figure 6.1.

The on-entry assessment made in language and mathematics were set in the context of children's social and emotional development. In formulating an assessment for personal and social learning the team had no National Curriculum document and no later assessments to consider. However, the central contextualizing importance of personal and social development made the task a priority for the team. There are many factors and strands in the personal and social development of young children. To present a consistent model, the team selected the three strands that seemed to have the greatest impact on children's achievement. The strands selected were settling in, response to setting, and attitude and approach to learning. Using the same five-point scale baseline descriptions were written that would enable practitioners to place children on a continuum and provide information to support the analysis of achievements in language and mathematics.

Figure 6.1: Baseline assessment descriptions

	Reading	Number	Attitude and approach to learning
1	No observable evidence — may only indicate a reluctance to share achievement.	No observable evidence — may only indicate a developing fluency in English and/or a reluctance to share achievement.	Observes rather than becoming involved in activities. Needs adult support to choose and move between areas and activities. Is reluctant to participate in any area.
2	Is fairly attentive to story in a 1–1 or small group situation with favourite story books. Shows an interest in illustration and some print in the environment. Recognizes own name, or initial letter of name with support.	Joins in with familiar number songs and rhymes. Counts aloud to 5, usually accurately. Counts to 5 using everyday objects arranged in a regular way, using 1–1 correspondence by either pointing to or moving the objects.	Often works alongside particular adults and peers. Will regularly work alone or in parallel play. Can select favourite activities and work for short periods. Is reliant on others to gain experiences.
3	Enjoys books and is beginning to select and handle them with care. Knows the difference between print and illustration and notices environmental print. Looks at books alone. Shares and discusses favourite books with others. Recognizes own name and associates sounds with some letters.	Takes part confidently in number songs and rhymes. Plays simple number games with support. Counts aloud to 10, usually accurately. Counts to 10 using everyday objects arranged in a regular way. Recognizes and uses numbers to 5, with some support.	Can select from a wide range of activities and work for a reasonable time, co-operating with adults and peers. Undertakes most classroom routines independently. Is developing positive attitudes to many aspects of work in the classroom.
4	Enjoys and handles books with care and responds to story with comments on plot and character. Knows that print remains constant and conveys meaning. Using a range of cues 'reads' known texts with accuracy. Reads own name and some familiar words. Recognizes the letters of the alphabet by shape and sound.	Plays simple number games independently. Counts to 10 using everyday objects arranged either in a regular or random way, usually correctly. Is familiar with some larger numbers from everyday life. Recognizes, orders and uses written numbers to 10. Shows an awareness of number operations.	Can select activities and resources independently. Is able to sustain concentration and to seek help when needed. Is readily involved in many activities and experiences in school. Is growing in confidence in approaching new work and situations.
5	Enjoys reading and sharing a wide range of reading materials. Responds to literature with preferences and opinions. Recognizes and reads familiar words in a simple text. Uses phonic and contextual clues. Reads to an adult from simple personal books and from published books.	Accurately counts, orders, adds and subtracts numbers to 10, using apparatus, and can estimate with some success. Reads, writes and orders written numbers to 10. Shows an interest in larger numbers, counting and reading numbers to 20 and beyond, and showing some awareness of place value.	Is interested and actively involved in most experiences and aspects of school life. Is able to concentrate for extended periods and persevere until tasks are completed. Is enthusiastic, self-motivated and eager to learn.

Source: A Framework for Entry Assessment, Leeds City Council Department of Education, 1997
(The baseline descriptions have been formulated to link with the 'Desirable Outcomes for Children's Learning on Entering Compulsory Education' and the requirements of the National Curriculum Programmes of Study, Attainment Targets and Level Descriptions.)

- 1 Indicates that the teacher has not observed evidence of achievement at this stage.
- 2 Indicates the early stages of development. The child is gaining experience.
- 3 Indicates some evidence of achievement in the SCAA Desirable Outcomes for Children's Learning and that he or she is building on experience.
- 4 Indicates attainment at the level of the SCAA Desirable Outcomes for Children's Learning and that there are elements of achievement which indicate work towards Level 1.
- 5 Indicates attainment beyond the SCAA Desirable Outcomes for Children's Learning and that a range of competencies and skills at Level 1 of the National Curriculum are being demonstrated.

The overall approach to baseline assessment aimed to promote good assessment practice and encode observed evidence of achievement for statistical purposes, allowing numerical outcomes to be generated by qualitative means.

How was the *Framework for Entry Assessment* implemented?

The implementation of *A Framework for Entry Assessment* across the Authority proved to be a task of unanticipated scale. The commitment of the LEA was central to the success of that implementation. The close relationships and collegial approaches of the early years team operating within the structure of that solid commitment meant that unrealistic deadlines and time scales were more or less met.

Advisory and Inspection Services launched the *Framework for Entry Assessment* on an audience of schools that was expectant and eagerly awaiting its arrival. Early years practitioners had been working and reflecting upon the qualitative aspects of this crucial process for some time. Headteachers, through their local forum, had been requesting baseline measures with numerical outcomes that would contextualize later standardized assessments in school. Although the focus of their interests diverged, practitioners and managers in schools alike were keen to embrace the new initiative. The local Authority acknowledged the concerns and viewpoints of both groups while keeping an eye firmly on the emerging national imperatives. The statistical data needed by the Authority to inform decisions aimed at raising achievement was to be generated by encoding observation-led assessment that would respect young children as learners and acknowledge the context of learning as crucial. The *Framework* met a need identified by a wide community of practice, from the advisory services through to the classroom.

A fast-moving national imperative coupled with the high numbers of early years practitioners within the city who were active in the development of the *Framework* made it difficult to limit the size of the pilot. Schools wanted to volunteer to be a part of the learning process of phase one. With no pressure and little advertisement 120 schools signed up to trial the materials and the assessment instrument. The Authority made no attempt to influence the sample or control the group for statistical purposes. The response bears witness to the commitment and enthusiasm of all concerned.

Due emphasis and priority was given to the initial training programme for managers and early years practitioners. For headteachers, deputies and assessment coordinators there was an introductory meeting followed by an intensive half-day session to raise awareness of the *Framework* and its implications for early years practice. The two-day training course for early years practitioners aimed to highlight and make close connection between qualitative assessment practice and best fit baseline judgments. Observation, profiling and report writing would inform the quantifiable judgments, that would be made on observable evidence of achievement in a range of contexts relevant to young learners.

The training was viewed as an evolving and developmental process that would be reflexive and responsive to emerging need from schools. Practitioners were not given rigid procedures to observe or perform, but were required to reflect upon current good practice and meet the requirements of baseline assessment by planning for any aspect of the process that critical enquiry deemed a priority for development. Reflective practitioners engaged with the *Framework* in an interactive and interlocking way. The Early Years Advisory Team responded with a flexible support package that met particular needs as and when they emerged. That package ranged from drop-in surgeries and telephone helplines to a series of more focused training courses to develop qualitative assessment practices such as observation skills, the partnership with parents and summative reporting. The atmosphere among early years practitioners and advisory teachers at this time was exhilarating as the wider implications within the Framework begun to emerge. Challenge was inherent in the qualitative and the quantitative process but the focus on observation-led assessment was leading many practitioners to reflect critically upon their provision and practice and actively seek improvement. The nature of the assessment was impacting upon practice in the classroom and raising the dialogue between nursery and reception practitioners about what constituted an appropriate curriculum for young learners. The need to gather observable evidence of achievement in a range of contexts was posing questions about the levels of resourcing and staffing that had not been predicted at the onset of the project. Teachers observing children closely in the first few weeks in the reception class were not only experiencing the joys of interaction but also reaching a better appreciation of the rich complexity of young children's knowledge and understanding. Many reception teachers acknowledged that fuller understanding and the way that it better informed the planning for the individual child and for the provision in the classroom. However, for some the experience was less rewarding, as they struggled to make accurate judgments with neither the appropriate resources nor sufficient staff to interact in meaningful learning experiences or activities. The requirements of baseline assessment were highlighting clearly the issues of early admission to reception classes.

For many nursery practitioners who had been active in the development of the Framework there was an imperative to find a clear voice in the process to ensure that young children's previous experiences were valued and properly accounted for. Here the growth area was in sharing achievements through summaries of learning; the result was more defined and clearly focused observation and the recognition of the need to analyse the evidence so diligently gathered. This would lead for many to the improved identification of significant learning and closer monitoring of pupil progress in self-initiated activity. It highlighted the many opportunities to promote literacy and numeracy in children's self chosen activity in areas of play provision and focused teacher thinking on the strategies that would exploit this further.

The 120 schools involved in phase one of the initiative gave of their best to the project. All completed the process and transmitted data on optical mark reader sheets to the Assessment and Achievement Unit by the date specified. The information was processed and the resultant data was returned to schools within four weeks. The implementation of the Framework for Entry Assessment was hard work, but stimulating and exciting. Many of the challenges and tensions were predicted and allowed for in the training and preparation, but others were unexpected and underestimated. The *Framework* was proving to be an agent for change.

Meanwhile the national agenda continued to move rapidly. Baseline assessment would be a statutory requirement, but there would be a national framework of accredited baseline assessment schemes rather than a national system. The data from phase one was persuasive and convinced the LEA of the need to go for accreditation and to encourage the remaining 120 schools within the authority to join the Leeds Framework.

What factors supported the successful implementation of the Framework?

Phase one of the initiative was evaluated by questionnaire to the headteachers and the practitioners, and by monitoring through advisory time in school. This evaluation process indicated many factors that supported effective implementation of the Framework. In most cases the success was rooted tin the reflective practice of teachers and headteachers. Their desire to make the process work for children led to careful planning and sensible decision making. Headteachers, deputies and assessment or Key Stage coordinators played a significant role in successful implementation of the Framework. Senior managers were encouraged to attend training and consider the wider implications and whole school issues involved in baseline assessment. Schools that accessed training for managers frequently had planned approaches to implementing baseline assessment in order to give good support to staff in reception classes. This raised the status of the assessment instrument and the early years teams, showing value for their work. Implementation was supported if schools had enabled the release of all early years staff to attend the training programme. Many schools had taken the opportunity to train teachers, nursery nurses and teaching assistants together wherever possible. If this substantial commitment was followed through by procedures that promoted dialogue between early years staff, then the quality of the assessment process was enhanced and the reliability of the data was better assured.

The schools with well established, good qualitative assessment practice naturally found the process easier. They had the observable evidence of achievement already noted and in some cases the mechanisms for sharing information with parents, carers and receiving teachers were already in place. For such schools making baseline judgments brought a heightened focus to those vital first weeks in school. Many of the most skilled and experienced practitioners found that the deadline pressure of baseline judgments brought additional clarity to their knowledge and understanding of each child and an intensity to the planning of an appropriate curriculum programme to meet the needs identified. Those settings that fully appreciated the importance of observation-led assessment found the process less daunting, but also acknowledged the need for additional focus. The result in some nursery and reception classes was a neater, sharpened process of gathering evidence and development planning to improve the range of qualitative assessment procedures.

Baseline judgments are more likely to be a reliable reflection of on-entry achievement if the child's previous experiences have been valued. A developing dialogue between and collaborative approaches with all adults who may have knowledge of the child was a clear success criteria. Schools that promoted dialogue made baseline judgments that were safer overall and better rooted in observed evidence and collected information.

Judgments that were supported by written evidence in records of achievement, profiles or summative reports from previous providers also proved to be more reliable, especially when the records were focused rather than anecdotal and supported by improved liaison between the settings concerned.

Observation-led assessment is a key aspect that runs through the whole qualitative process within the Framework. The placing of observable evidence of achievement at the centre of the quantitative stage proved problematic for those reception classes unable to provide a rich and wide range of contexts. Staff working in classrooms with limited space, support or appropriate resources found the process challenging. This was often compounded in classrooms that were not organized in a way that encouraged pupil independence or where child-initiated activity was not supported by adult interaction and sensitive intervention. Where pupils self select from a range of relevant and meaningful learning experiences staff have a chance of observing children closely. Without autonomous pupils staff are left in supervisory or managerial roles in the classroom supporting adult-directed activity. Successful implementation of the Framework acknowledged the nature of 4-year-olds as learners and their need to do lots and talk about it. It also benefited from teachers who conceptualized themselves as supporters of children's thinking and learning rather than as instructors or transmitters of knowledge. This resulted for some in a tension that is well mirrored currently in the national debate about what constitutes an appropriate curriculum for young learners. Well established early years principles underpinned the approach to good practice promoted within the Framework, but they are not universally adhered to or unchallenged.

In what ways can baseline assessment data be interpreted and used?

Early years practitioners would rephrase this question and ask in what ways the data could be made to work for children. Most involved in the implementation of the Framework had been enthusiastic about the process, yet many now retained a curious ambivalence towards the numerical outcomes that the base-line measures had generated. For some this reluctance to engage with the data was rooted in deep concerns about the use such data could and might be put to. A typical response was to make light of the data. For others the data represented a mechanism for evaluation too far alienated from their usual approaches to monitoring practice. After a flush of initial interest practitioners were left wondering what all the fuss was about. However, in a climate where increasing faith in the validity of comparative data prevailed, it was clear that further support and training on the use and interpretation of such data was essential.

The Assessment and Achievement Unit rightly believed that, in the first instance, schools required limited data that was easily interpreted. This lesson had been learnt working with the secondary sector, where an avalanche of assessment information had not supported schools planning effectively for improvement. With the baseline data, sophistication would come with time and in response to clearly identified need or obvious use. Schools received an initial package that included the aggregated data for the city, the data for their school and a straightforward sheet to support an initial analysis. Using this schools were encouraged to compare generic data and aggregates with those of the city. This simple device aimed to raise practitioner awareness of the potential of comparative analysis by questioning the data and looking for any issues that might arise. For example, a high number of children placed in category one or two for speaking and listening would have implications for the teaching of reading in the reception class. In phase two the initial package also included individual pupil data and a small booklet that supported further analysis using prompts to ask a widening range of questions that focused on individual pupils and action to take.

The data package was swiftly followed up by training sessions for managers and early years staff on interpreting and using baseline assessment data. This training supported schools in the cautious and tentative interrogation of data received, and provided an opportunity to share the wider range of interesting data available to the local Authority.

This second wave of data looked at broad issues across the LEA such as gender, ethnicity, free school meals, previous experience and month of birth. In some cases this data caused surprises, but in many it confirmed long held beliefs. The data confirmed the impact of month of birth on achievement and gender differences in relation to reading. For every pattern or trend in the LEA data there were schools presenting as exceptions. Schools, once aware of these patterns, were encouraged to see if the pattern or trend was repeated in their data. At the heart of this interrogation is the pursuit of improvement. If change is to occur LEAs and schools need to use this information to share good practice and ideas, consider provision, resources and organization, and identify training and support needs. The initial process must be one of reflection and questioning not of fast response or quick fix. Trends or patterns over time might provoke the search for appropriate pragmatic responses.

The personal and social dimension to the baseline assessment measures was of immediate interest, and prompted many schools to a close consideration of admission, transition and behaviour policies. It stimulated dialogue about how raising self-esteem and positive attitudes to learning could become a specific and planned for educational objective. The personal and social data provoked many to examine the reality of the partnership with parents and make plans for improvement. Some schools made changes to their policy of staggered admissions to admit the younger and less experienced children first to support their settling in to school life. Others reconsidered organizational demands made on young learners such as attending assembly, large group story sessions as a forum for speaking and listening, playtime and the lunch hour. Many increased the level and scope of their communications with parents, and expressed the intention of using the baseline descriptions to provide a context for understanding the achievements of learners on into Key Stage 1.

High on the agenda in these training sessions for both school managers and practitioners was a warning on the possible consequences of overinterpretation or overreaction on a school or individual pupil level. In some schools, small sample sizes made predictive and comparative use not viable on other than an individual pupil basis. All schools needed to exercise caution in the interpretation of data in the pilot years. The data supports the validity of the baseline descriptions as an assessment instrument that reflects a range of achievements young learners demonstrate on entry to full time school, in language, mathematics and social and emotional development. The sample population of the city is sufficiently large to enable minor flaws and inconsistencies in the baseline judgments to balance each other. However, until practitioners are secure and confident, and more experienced in making and moderating baseline judgments, the data will not be entirely reliable.

While there were many aspects that were clearly successful there is still much to develop and refine within the administration and processing arrangements, but more importantly in the moderation process that will over time ensure the consistency of teacher assessments and judgments.

When considering the interpretation and use of baseline data, it is essential to retreat from the percentages and the numbers and reconsider the needs of real children in actual classrooms. Staff in nursery classes can meaningfully question the data to identify any strong trends or results and plan for the provision they will make. In the spirit of reflective practice the data can support the monitoring and evaluation of the curriculum programme and the identification of areas for development. Subsequent data can form part of the success criteria for any action or development planning. Many nursery classes have responded with innovative initiatives aimed at raising on-entry achievement through enriched and enhanced provision. The success of the Framework is embedded in the good qualitative practice of nursery practitioners.

Staff in reception classes can meaningfully question the data to inform their planning for the individual child and for learning experiences and opportunities. The baseline descriptions themselves provide a framework for monitoring pupil progress through the remainder of the reception year. Many reception practitioners made assessments using the descriptors at the end of the reception year to show the progress made and inform the planning of year one colleagues. The process of making baseline judgments, particularly in the using and applying of shape, space and measures strands in mathematics, highlighted for some reception practitioners the inadequacy of their resources and the need to provide the contexts in which the children could demonstrate achievement. If provisions such as sand, water, blocks, large construction or box modelling are not readily or regularly available, the assessments were hard to make. Many have planned to change this. Anxiety about the plight of young 4-year-olds in reception classes is not a new phenomena, but this model of baseline assessment heavily underlines it.

What is the way forward?

The successful way forward will require staff to;

- value qualitative evidence;
- value children's previous experiences;
- improve the partnership with parents;
- consider an appropriate curriculum programme for young learners;
- combat under-estimation;
- use quantitative data cautiously but positively.

Valuing qualitative evidence

Quantitative data is not more valuable than qualitative data. The value of data rests in its accuracy and usefulness, not in the volume of figures or percentages. Yet these are testing times and the tendency is to place too great an emphasis on the numerical outcomes despite widespread acceptance of the potential use and misuse of statistics. In this Framework, the baseline measures are not the most important part of the process. Experience would suggest that achievements that are readily quantified are not always significant, and that significant learning often eludes easy detection and measurement. The process of quantifying often simplifies and may compromise the complexity that is in the detail. Although these broad brush strokes are useful, the evidence that best informs planning for the individual or the educational programme is in the qualitative detail. Quantitative data must be set within a qualitative context if it is to work in the interests of children. Bare data, over-rationalized, and in the hands of managers and inspectors is of limited real value.

Valuing children's previous experiences

The baseline process is not the sole domain of reception teachers nor is it limited to the first seven weeks of term. Reception class teachers should need and value information and evidence that will support their baseline decisions — anything less risks avoidable underestimation.

Improving the partnership with parents

Improving the partnership with parents is a way forward rich in potential for raising achievement. Early years practitioners have long worked to nurture meaningful dialogue with parents; it has often proved difficult to sustain in schools. The Framework acknowledges this key element and encourages schools to consider further strategies that will maintain and enrich that critical partnership. Many schools are developing procedures for home visits, meetings, open sessions, more extended prior visiting, contacts with local nurseries and play groups and more social occasions. Most schools are increasing the opportunities for a variety of meetings that share children's achievements with parents, carers and the children themselves. Parental contributions to profile systems and reports are encouraged and summative report writing is an early years growth area. This trend has a clear resonance with the government's imperative to involve and help parents to participate in their child's learning.

Considering an appropriate curriculum programme for young learners

The central place of observation-led assessment within the Framework has highlighted the importance of continuous provision as an appropriate context for young children to demonstrate their achievements. Well planned and well resourced areas of provision can form the foundation of an appropriate early years curriculum, allowing open ended activity that differentiates by outcome, and the child some control over the rate, pace and scope of their learning. The issues connected with the early admission to reception classes, where the needs of the child might not have been paramount, are well documented (Bennett and Kell, 1989; Cleave and Brown, 1991; Osborn and Millbank, 1987). When inappropriate provision has made achievement difficult to observe, it frequently leads to testing situations as the only option. The likely result is underestimation, and when underestimation frames the beginning of a child's full time education, underachievement is the likely outcome.

Combating underestimation

Combating underestimation and raising expectations may prove to be the most positive outcome of this project. Raising expectations was implicit rather than explicit in the process, but represents a very desirable outcome. Substantial research suggests that the capabilities of young learners may be regularly underestimated (Donaldson, 1978; Hughes, 1986; Tizard and Hughes, 1984). Their experimental findings suggest that children can do and understand beyond usual expectation if the context is meaningful. The work of Vygotsky is beginning to have an impact among those who work with young children. He suggests that practitioners should consider the capabilities of the learners in terms of what they can achieve independently, and what they can achieve with the help and support of an interested adult. What might be in the latter category today, may be moved to the former tomorrow (Vygotsky, 1962, 1978). These ideas offer practitioners a powerful and proactive role in the learning of young children, and will influence thinking about the nature of classroom interaction and the possibilities for a more interventionist approach.

When the work of these psychologists is coupled with the increasing and emphatic data that clearly indicates the importance of early learning in later educational and social success, the potential for change and improvement in the hands of reflective practitioners is great (Ball, 1994; Osborn and Millbank, 1987). Accurate baseline data can help raise achievement by providing reliable evidence to inform the planning of an appropriately challenging curriculum.

Using quantitative data cautiously but positively

The way forward must be in the cautious and tentative inclusion of baseline quantitative data into the qualitative process as another piece of evidence that will inform planning for improvement. It should represent one of several mechanisms for monitoring effectiveness.

The issue of deliberate underestimation to enhance value-added analysis at the end of Key Stage 1 was challenged directly in training. Schools were asked to consider that any enhancement gained could not be replicated at the end of Key Stage 2 without substantially oversupporting the children in Year 6. A school could only make Key Stage 1 look impressive at the expense of colleagues in Key Stage 2. It is a sad reflection on the state of primary education that the anxiety caused by league tables could result in strategies so far removed from the good of the child. It is in the interests of children to combat complacency and underachievement, but if the measures considered result in schools moving away from the best interests of the child, it is time to return to some first principles.

The purpose of any assessment is to provide rich and reliable evidence to inform teachers' planning. The need for reliability requires the LEA to support the process of the moderation. The Framework relies on the value of quality teacher assessment which will grow with time, patience, dialogue and confidence. This gradual process can be supported by structures that enable cooperation and collaboration in moderation networks, and encourage the development of quality exemplification materials and portfolios.

If policy is to effectively develop practice and truly enrich the learning experiences and lives of children, it is essential that the way forward must keep faith with the principles that underpin good early years practice.

Principles Underpinning Young Children's Learning (Taken from *A Framework for Entry Assessment*, City of Leeds Education Authority, Appendix One)

Each child is unique with individual needs, individual ways of learning and different rates of learning.

Young children learn most effectively when:

- they are actively involved and interested;
- they are in a meaningful context;
- they are supported by interested and informed adults;
- the experiences offered are relevant to their immediate interests;
- their previous experiences/achievements are valued and used as a starting point for their education;
- they are encouraged to have a positive self-image and high self-esteem;
- they have some control over their learning;
- parents/carers are involved.

References

BALL, C. (1994) *Start Right: The Importance of Early Learning*, London: RSA.

BENNETT, N. and KELL, J. (1989) *A Good Start: Four-Year-Olds in Infant Schools*, Oxford: Basil Blackwell.

CLEAVE, S. and BROWN, S. (1991) *Early to School: Four-Year-Olds in Infant Classes*, Windsor: NFER-Nelson.

DONALDSON, M. (1978) *Children's Minds*, London: Fontana.

HUGHES, M. (1986) *Children and Number*, Oxford: Basil Blackwell.

LEEDS EDUCATION (1997) *A Framework for Entry Assessment*, Leeds: Leeds City Council Education Department.

OSBORN, A.F. and MILLBANK, J.E. (1987) *The Effects of Early Education*, Oxford: Clarendon Press.

SCHOOL CURRICULUM AND ASSESSMENT AUTHORITY (1996) *Desirable Outcomes for Children's Learning on Entering Compulsory Education*, London: DfEE/SCAA.

SCHOOL CURRICULUM AND ASSESSMENT AUTHORITY (1997) *The National Framework for Baseline Assessment*, London: SCAA.

TIZARD, B. and HUGHES, M. (1984) *Young Children Learning: Talking and Listening at Home and at School*, London: Fontana.

VYGOTSKY, L.S. (1962) *Thought and Language*, Cambridge, MA: MIT Press.

VYGOTSKY, L.S. (1978) *Mind in Society*, Cambridge, MA: Harvard University Press.

7　Using Data to Drive Up Standards: Statistics or Psychology?

Peter Dudley

There is a widely held belief that looking at data improves learning and achievement. For instance, one of the most common OFTSED Key Issues for primary schools usually reads something like: 'In order to improve standards, subject coordinators need to monitor attainment and progress in their subjects and evaluate the quality of teaching and learning.' Ironic really when the team of people who reached this conclusion have usually just spent the best part of a week doing precisely the same themselves. Paying attention to pupil data, however, has rightly become a cornerstone of a national policy to drive up standards. This has led to a succession of developments in the use of assessment data, alongside the development of a range of approaches to gathering and using other forms of data in quantitative ways — from inspection judgments to pupil attitude surveys. In the past this would more likely have been presented qualitatively through words rather than statistically, using numbers, percentages and averages.

Central to the success of the strategies proposed in the white paper *Excellence in Schools* (DfEE, 1997a) is the ability of schools to use pupil data to boost achievement. 'The use within a school of reliable and consistent performance analyses enables teachers to assess progress by their pupils and to change their teaching strategies accordingly' (p. 27). The white paper indicates that a key measure of an LEA's effectiveness will be its ability to 'provide clear performance data that can be readily used by schools' to set targets for improvement in pupil achievement.' (p. 27). The 1998 education act will set out an agenda of data analysis and target setting for schools which is likely to be a key element of school activity and a major determinant of education strategy for the coming decade at least. In this chapter I intend to examine some of the problems which this policy may encounter in the early days, unless sufficient attention is paid to the psychological lessons we need to learn about how best to present, analyse and use data and targets within schools.

I will consider the following propositions:

- there is a need to change preconceptions of what the word 'data' signifies and to widen our views of what we mean by 'performance data';
- in managing its use within school, we need to understand the psychology of data — how people respond to data and how data affect people's actions and motivations;

- there are strategies for managing the analysis, presentation and discussion of data within school which help ensure positive change takes place as a result;
- education in Britain has always turned to data about the past and is only just beginning to come to terms with data about the future;
- the success of target setting as an improvement strategy is entirely dependent on a positive psychology;
- we need to explore what organizational or societal 'zones of proximal development' look like in a learning organization or a learning society.

The need to change our preconceptions of what the word 'data' means

'Data' is a word with which many teachers feel uncomfortable. When asked what it conjures up in peoples' minds, the following replies are common: 'numbers', 'computers', 'graphs', 'confusion' and of course 'star trek'! While the word 'data' continues to have such an effect, many may avoid confronting data issues. There is a gulf between these notions of data and the teaching strategies; we need to consider changing in the light of the analysis of data (DfEE, 1997a: 27). We need first, to build a recognition that data exist in many forms and that pupils' work and teachers' plans are data and are as important in the picture of school and pupil performance as numbers or charts generated from surveys or assessments.

In managing its use, we need to understand the psychology of data

Data do not always generate actions. This is sometimes because those who need to act do not know of the data's existence. Sometimes it is because the data are not viewed as being in any way valid by those being asked to respond. Published tables of raw examination results are a good example of this latter form of data. They have been dismissed as unfair year after year by the teaching profession but ironically one of the main effects has been to boost a proliferation of 'value-added' data and the industry surrounding its creation.

In fact, value-added data provides a powerful illustration of the power data can have when it is linked to an equally powerful psychology. Value-added projects have often involved groups of schools voluntarily sharing comparative data. Factors over which the schools have little or no control such as pupils' prior attainment or background are removed from the measurement made of each school's effectiveness. Value-added data focus on pupil *progress* rather than finishing points and compare similar schools with each other in terms of the relative progress of groups of similar pupils. In this way, a school in which pupils make a lot of progress can have this recognized through the value-added data even though the school may be a long way down a raw results league table.

For these reasons value-added analyses have proved popular with teachers and managers. This, I believe, is because teachers perceive them to be fair. As a result of this acceptance, value-added data have sufficiently impacted on 'changing teaching strategies'. This, in turn, has brought about acceptance of their value at policy level leading to the introduction of national value-added information from 1999 onwards.

> The concept of 'value added' . . . has made a significant impact on schools, particularly in helping staff realise the need to track and monitor pupil progress and not just concentrate on outcomes. This has led to intelligent schools developing a wide range of strategies to monitor progress . . . (MacGilchrist, Myers and Reed, 1997: 2)

While critics of value-added data argue that it can be used to explain away failure by blaming social factors, it is, undeniably, uniquely powerful in the way teachers and managers are prepared to trust the data and act on them. Value added is therefore valid in a number of ways. First, because people are prepared to act on the basis of the data, it is a positive force in bringing improvement in pupil achievement. It therefore has a strong 'validity of "consequence"' (Messick, 1989: 10).

Second, in measuring pupil progress rather than merely learning outcome, value-added data are perceived by teachers and school managers to be measuring what is *a reasonable outcome of effective teaching*, measuring 'what is valuable rather than valuing what is easily measured' as the phrase goes (US Government, 1991). As such, it has a strong 'construct validity' (Messick, 1989: 7). The fact that value-added has grown in popularity and currency among users of its own accord, indicates that not only does it have ecological validity (Black and Wiliam, 1998: 8), but also and more powerfully still, it provokes a 'yes, of course' rather than a 'yes, but' experience (Kidder, 1982 in Lather 1986: 271) associated with 'face validity' (p. 271).

I would argue that value-added data enjoy this validity and currency almost entirely because of such psychological *affective* factors as trust and perceived fairness. They are clearly important ingredients in any data set intended to bring about changes in teaching strategies. To put it another way, an analysis which does not iron these out may not so readily be embraced or acted upon.

Are there ways of managing the analysis, presentation and discussion of data within school which help ensure positive change takes place as a result?

In order to gain some insights into this question, I studied the reactions of groups of teachers in four schools to pupil perception data. The data were presented in histograms showing the responses of pupils to items in a survey of their perceptions of themselves as learners. Such surveys have been promoted as contributing to school improvement. 'Schools which participate in the surveys are able to see how their school relates to national averages . . . These results enable schools to refine their improvement strategies and target resources appropriately' (Barber, 1994: 8). The purpose of the study was to find out what responses such data provoke and how they relate to change strategies.

Good news data and bad news data

The study investigated the idea of data sets containing good news and bad news, that is, information that is supportive of practice in the school or critical of it. An initial assumption had been to suspect that if the news within the data was positive then it was more likely to be accepted than if the news was negative. However, although the analysis confirmed the existence of good news and bad news data, these other assumptions were challenged (Dudley, 1997). Responses to the data sets fell between four Response Categories.

Response categories

1. Action response — active critical acceptance of the issue behind the data	3. Passive uncritical rejection of the issue within the data
2. Passive uncritical acceptance of the issue in the data	4. Active, critical rejection of the issue within the data

These are illustrated in the following examples taken from transcripts of people responding to pupil perception data.

1. Action responses are characterized by consideration, debate and reflection on the issue behind the data

I would have expected more to say 'Yes I do worry' than have come out here . . . I had quite a few children who said 'Oh they're being nasty because my work was too good

Sometimes comparisons are made with other information or data and strategies for action are suggested.

Where I was before they used to have a sharing book as well as a reading book so that every night each child had a book to read in bed and that's something we can . . .

it would be interesting to find out what strategy [another school in the chart is using] . . . it would be interesting to find out exactly what they were doing next wouldn't it

it would be very interesting to compare it to . . . I wonder what they're offering that we're not? (p. 50)

2. Passive uncritical acceptance of the issue behind the data is welcomed or accepted without reflection, debate or question:

- 'That's good'
- 'and look at the one at the back as well'
- 'Mmmmm'

or people acclimatize to the data rather than challenging it:

In an ideal world it would be a hundred % — but then . . . there'll always be those children . . .

3. Passive uncritical rejection of the data is typified by a tendency to generalize or rationalize the message behind the data:

- 'That doesn't surprise me really. Does it you?'
- 'No'

or a rejection of the test or method:

- 'It just reflects the time of year that it [the data collection] was done.'

4. A critical rejection of the message behind the data will put the data under pressure and explore the issue as determinedly as occurs with an action response before rejecting the issue.

Significantly, the analysis of teachers' responses revealed that,

1. an action response is only 10 per cent more likely to be generated by good news data than by bad news data;
2. action responses are not associated particularly strongly either with surprises or with predictable news;
3. the message behind the data tends to be mentally 'filed away' when it is perceived as good news but not challenged or reflected upon;
4. data are likely to be 'binned' and not acted upon when they are seen as predictable bad news.

Where points 1 and 2 perhaps have positive implications for the development of the use of pupil assessment data, points 3 and 4 present problems. Point 4 is unsurprising but highlights the need for strategies to help create a positive action response to data which one can predict is likely to be bad news. Point 3 raises the difficulty of generating a positive action-oriented response to improvement in a situation which is perceived as not being problematic — the 'if it ain't broke why fix it' syndrome.

It is natural to look for problems within data but importantly, if schools are to improve, critical examination of successes — of what seems to work — must become as commonplace as investigating what seems to be going wrong. This raises a problem for the notion of 'teacher as researcher'. The development of subject leaders and middle managers with whole school responsibilities is leading primary schools increasingly to take on a shared responsibility for the research which happens within school following monitoring and analysis of pupil level data. Stenhouse's (1981) vision of the teacher as researcher (p. 109) therefore needs to shift now towards one of *school* as researcher.

Can we engineer positive action-oriented responses to pupil data?

An analysis of what contributed to the nature of the response to the data revealed that there were common features in the discussions about the data sets which were associated with each of the four types of response. These were:

- *Teaching and learning* — where the discussion included specific reference to classroom or pedagogical situations;
- *Policy* — where the discussion made reference to the school's policy on a certain issue;
- *Gender* — where the discussion made reference to issues of gender;
- *Home* — where the discussion included reference either to parents, home background or socio-economic issues;
- *Comparison* — where use was made in the discussion of comparative evidence of outcomes in other schools;
- *Method* — where an aspect of the methodology such as item wording or the timing of the instrument were criticized or discussed;
- *Preparation* — where it is clear that preparation for reading the data through use of the preparation exercise contributed to the discussion.

This suggests that careful preparation for reading data and discussion while reading the data which relates to classrooms, to teaching and learning along with the ability to make comparisons with the data from other schools, all seem to increase the potential for the response to the data to be critical, positive and action-oriented.

Conversely, where the discussion is around factors over which the school has little direct influence the response is less likely to be critical, positive or action-oriented. These factors may also tend to relate to home background, parents or gender issues. The situation may occur where the potential implications of the data outcome have not been sufficiently thought through (by advance preparation for reading the data) or where the kinds of strategies which could be employed in response to the data have not been considered.

The following important points emerge to help guide the management of pupil data:

- Crucial issues within data can easily be lost.
- It is possible to manage the way people respond to performance data to help keep issues from being lost and to generate a critical but positive response.

The analysis suggests that positive responses to issues within data will increase with:

- the availability of comparative data;
- preparation for reading the data;
- prompts focusing discussion of pupil data on teaching, learning and issues which the school can influence as well as developing speculation skills;
- prior knowledge within the discussion group of a range of strategies for action or change;
- the introduction of ground rules into the discussion to ensure that apparent good news or reactions to perceived external influences such as 'home background' are sufficiently challenged.

Figure 7.1 maps the relationships between the discussion features, the issues or factors associated with them and their potential outcomes on to a four-point axis each point of which represents one of the four main response types.

It is important to examine some of the reasons why these associations occurred. This returns us to a consideration of the affective issues which play a role in determining how data are used. The ideas in Figure 7.1 can be reformulated into Figure 7.2.

This exploratory matrix would suggest that the more teachers discussing data are able to maintain some critical detachment from the issue while remaining confident about change and change strategies, the less likely the issue is to be lost.

Figure 7.1: *Ways teachers initially react to issues apparent in pupil perception data*

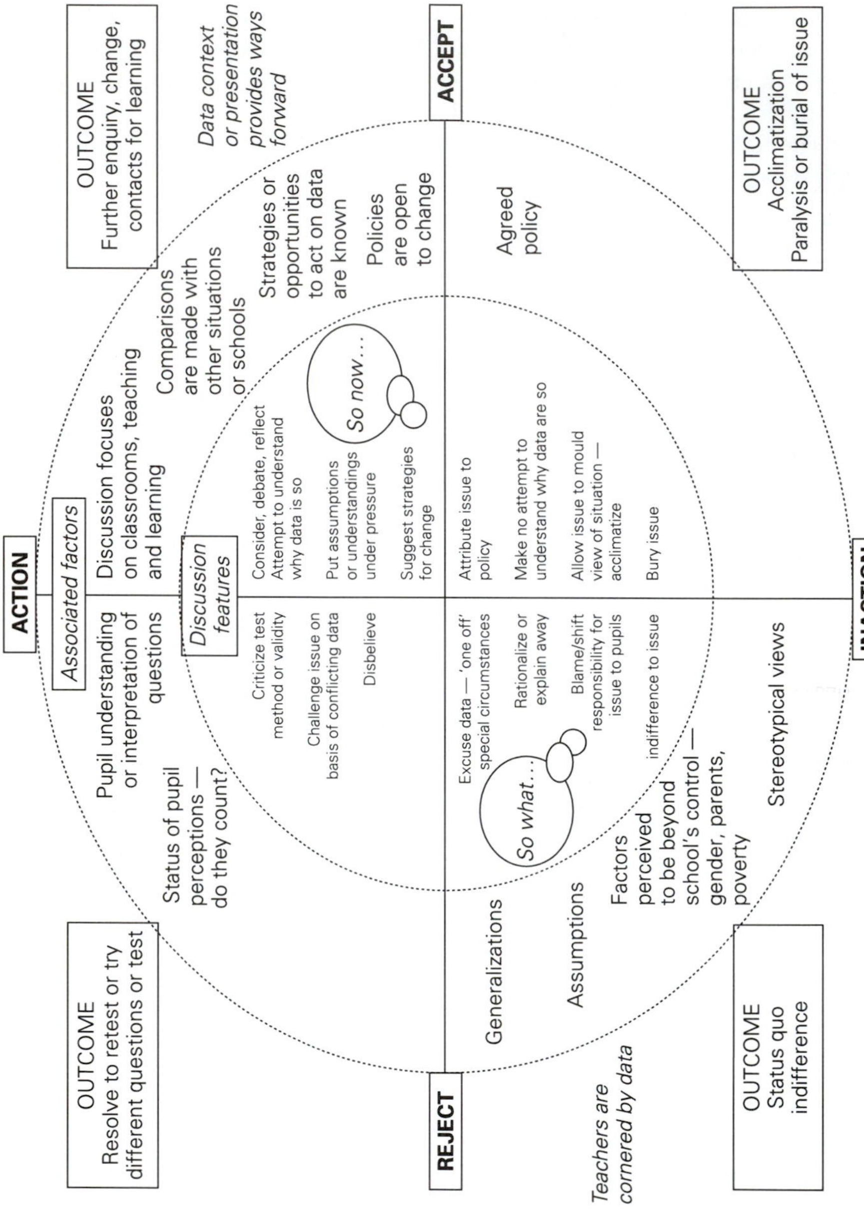

Figure 7.2: *Why people react to data in the ways they do*

Critical detachment from issue

		LOW	HIGH
Confidence with change and change strategies	LOW	personalization of issue paralysis 'devastation' acclimatization to data	criticize instrument generating data (e.g. test, assessment or survey) blame impact of external factors acclimatize to the data accepting the message uncritically and passively
	HIGH	rationalization of issue excusing issue explaining away issue	externalization of issue reflection and enquiry comparison and ideas transfer suggest strategies and action

It would be appropriate for managers in schools therefore, to prepare for the discussion of data by addressing the following questions with those who are likely to be involved in the discussion (Panel 1).

Panel 1. Questions teachers and managers need to consider in preparation for considering pupil data

- What aspects of these data are particularly important for the school?
- What aspects of these data are particularly important for me?
- Ideally, what would I expect the outcome to be?
- Realistically, what do I expect the outcome to be?
- What change or improvement strategies can we identify in advance of the discussion in order to promote positive action and avoid being cornered by bad news?
- Have we guarded against making assumptions about home background factors and taking steps to challenge such assumptions when they arise?

The following points need consideration in the light of any school's current approach to using pupil or assessment data.

How do we usually consider data now?

- Do we consider data informally or formally — do we have ground rules, a policy or any form of 'approach' that we take as a school?
- Do we go through any formal individual or collective preparation for considering pupil data?
- Do we have a shared view of expected outcomes or action?
- How could we improve the way we prepare to read data in the future?

Data about the past and data about the future

The introduction of targets for school improvement has created a new form of data. We have some experience of assessment data as data about learning and attainment which have already taken place. These are clearly data about the past. The notion of school and pupil targets brings us into consideration of assessment and attainment data which are about the future.

I remember only two years ago in 1996 hearing a well known colleague refer to primary schools as 'data free zones'. Now, barrage after barrage of data is fired off annually at primary schools in the efforts by government agencies such as QCA and OFTSED, LEAs, HE institutions and school improvement projects to demonstrate that they are playing their parts in helping schools to ask and maybe even begin to answer the well rehearsed questions 'How well are we doing?' and 'How do we compare with similar schools?' (DfEE, 1996). Consequently, within a matter of weeks, primary schools received the following sets of data about past learning and achievement:

- published performance tables of Key Stage 2 results;
- local LEA analyses and in some cases value-added and other comparative data;
- QCA Benchmarking information for Key Stages 1 and 2.
- PANDAs (Performance and Attainment Summaries)

as well as the following data about the future:

- national targets for literacy and numeracy;
- local LEA targets for literacy;
- LEA calculations of indicative target ranges for each school. (Thornton, 1998)

The success of target setting as a national improvement policy is dependent on positive psychology

Some may argue that setting a target is itself positive psychology. If, however, similar psychological processes operate in target setting as they do in influencing how people respond to other performance data, then the process needs inspired management at every level if it is to succeed. DfEE guidance on target setting (DfEE, 1997b) describes zones within which schools involved in target-setting research have set targets (p. 14). Figure 7.3 sets out the zones and links them with the four types of responses to data identified above.

If, as this analysis suggests, the psychology of targets is similar to the psychology of data, we need to ensure at all times that the response is one of active critical acceptance of the target if the target is to motivate and have its intended effect. This is true at every level in the process whether it be teacher and pupil, management and teacher, governors and management, LEA and school or government and LEA.

Michael Barber sets out the relationships between affective factors governing motivation and achievement in Figure 7.4.

Figure 7.3: Target zones and responses to target data

Target zone (From Targets to Action, DfEE 1997: 14)	Possible features in common with data response study	Dara response likely to apply to target data
The historic zone — playing down or obscuring past achievement in order to set targets behind current levels which will already have been met	Targeted improvement represents status quo, indifference and may suggest a feeling that real change is beyond school's control	Passive uncritical rejection of target data
The comfort zone — readily achievable targets	The improvement suggests the school may have acclimatized to the target or may already be on course to meet this target as a result of past changes so that further change may not be necessary	Passive acceptance of target data
The challenge zone — targets represent a marked difference	The school has identified an area in need of real change — has considered, debated, reflected and put assumptions under pressure in order to explore strategies for improvement	Active critical acceptance of target data
The unlikely zone — 'it is not advisable to stay in this zone for too long — failure to meet targets that are too ambitious can disappoint and undermine improvement initiatives' (p. 16)	Target data is too challenging. Target is disputed or disbelieved — it fails to engage	Active rejection of target

Figure 7.4: Self esteem/expectations matrix

SELF ESTEEM

		Low	High
EXPECTATIONS	Low	(a) Failure	(b) Complacency
	High	(c) Demoralisation	(d) Success

Source: Barber, 1997: 183

Where pupil self-esteem and teacher/pupil expectations are high, the outcome should be success in learning. The dynamic is applicable both to individuals and institutions in the target-setting process. One could readily substitute 'school expectations' and 'teacher self-esteem' with the target-setting process and the outcomes would be similar, or likewise LEA expectations and schools' self-esteem.

For targets to be achieved, we need to manage the process at classroom, school, LEA and national levels in order that the box (d) dynamic is maintained. Targets in the unlikely zone will put the process into box (c) and targets in the comfort zone will lead to box (b). The ways to create the conditions for success — box (d) — are through establishing a culture which produces this particular affective mix. For a teacher working with an individual pupil this is achieved by doing what Pollard with Filer (1996) describe as: 'structuring of *affective* and intellectual support in the zone of proximal development' (Pollard, 1996: 97 — my emphasis).

At school and LEA level we need to apply a similar model of learning to the situation where we are working within school to set targets for improvement and view this as a learning process — albeit 'organisational learning' (Argyris and Schon, 1978). We need to understand first, what is involved in an organizational zone of proximal development and then second, how we can best 'structure affective support'. We may be able to learn further from the classroom pupil/teacher learning model. To do so would suggest that target setting will work best through:

- creating and maintaining a culture of risk sharing with schools and teachers where targets are imaginative, challenging and demanding of new skills and changes;
- creating a culture where inevitably things will go wrong during the process of working towards targets because mistakes are a necessary part of learning;
- setting targets which relate to pupil progress as well as outcomes;
- providing dedicated formative feedback on current performance set against previous bests in order to motivate and reinforce success while avoiding giving too much feedback based on performance in comparison with other learners

> 'task involving evaluation is more effective than ego involving evolution' (Black and Wiliam, 1998: 6)

If these are characteristics which make target setting effective in boosting pupil learning then perhaps we need to apply them in organizational learning.

We need to explore what societal or organizational 'zones of proximal development' look like in a learning organization or a learning society

Target setting has now been moved from being a successful strategy used in school improvement research to a national policy. The culture has shifted from the research culture in which schools, teachers and LEAs are learners, to a culture of public accountability. In the wake of the press treatment of recent years given to educational standards, failing schools and HMCI's regular comments on failing teachers, the pressures of publication on school targets are likely to push them into the 'comfort' zone and away from the imaginative risk sharing climate.

Early indications are that the affective mix may not be being achieved. In April 1998 *The Times Educational Supplement* reported a negative effect on school managers of the approach many LEAs are taking to setting targets under the heading: 'Councils set literacy targets "too high"' (Thornton, 1998: 9). All this presents a dilemma for a government which wants a 'learning society' with learning institutions and intelligent schools which continually view 'the ambitious targets' for literacy and numeracy with 'excitement and enthusiasm' (Barber, 1997: 261). If we want learning organizations, then in order to maximize their achievement we have to ensure from policy level downwards that they are treated as learners.

References

ARGYRIS, C. and SCHON, D. (1978) *Organizational Learning: A Theory of Action Perspective*, Reading, MA: Addison-Wesley.

BARBER, M. (1994) *Young People and Their Attitudes to School: An Interim Report of a Research Project in the Centre for Successful Schools*, Keele: University of Keele.

BARBER, M. (1997) *The Learning Game: Arguments for an Education Revolution*, London: Gollancz.

BLACK, P. and WILIAM, D. (1998) *Assessment and Classroom Learning*, London: School of Education, Kings College, University of London.

DfEE (1996) *Improving Schools Programme Information Leaflet*, London: Department for Education and Employment.

DfEE (1997a) *Excellence in Schools*, London: HMSO.

DfEE STANDARDS AND EFFECTIVENESS UNIT (1997b) *From Targets to Action: Guidance to Support Effective Target Setting in Schools*, London: Department for Education and Employment.

DUDLEY, P. (1997) 'How teachers respond to pupil data', Paper presented at the British Educational Research Association Annual Conference, University of York, 10–14 September 1997.

LATHER, P. (1986) 'Research as praxis', in *Harvard Educational Review*, **56**, (3), pp. 259–77.

MacGILCHRIST, B., MYERS, K. and REED, J. (1997) *The Intelligent School*, London: Paul Chapman Publishing.

MESSICK, S. (1989) 'Meaning and values in test validation: The science and ethics of assessment', *Educational Researcher*, **18**, (2), pp. 5–11.

POLLARD, A. with FILER, A. (1996) *The Social World of Children's Learning*, London: Cassell.

STENHOUSE, L. (1981) 'What counts as research?, *British Journal of Educational Studies*, **24**, (2), June, pp. 103–13.

THORNTON, K. (1988) 'Councils set literacy targets "too high"', in *The Times Educational Supplement, 17 April 1998*, p. 9.

US GOVERNMENT REPORT (1991) 'Education counts' in *School Improvement Newsletter*, Summer 1995, ISEIC, London: University of London Institute of Education.

8   Do Pupil Perception Surveys Work with Young Children?

Peter Dudley

Ask yourself this question. How is it that some effective primary schools continue to have an impact on pupil achievement when they are 16? Sammons (1993) found that pupils who attended particular primary schools in the School Matters Project (Mortimore et al., 1988), were likely to achieve at 16 significantly better results than they would had they attended less effective primary schools — whatever their prior attainment, gender, ethnic or cultural background, and whatever secondary schooling they experienced.

When you have thought about that question, make a list of things which you think those primary schools must have given their children. Most people list the following:

- motivation;
- high expectations and self-esteem;
- a belief that learning is important;
- the best possible literacy and numeracy skills;
- the ability to organize and learn independently;
- the confidence to take risks in learning and to view mistakes as a necessary part of the process — not as failure.

The interesting thing is how many of these relate not to cognitive learning processes but to how learners *feel* about themselves — as learners. These 'affective' factors are vital to the process of learning and achievement but have often been overlooked in recent years in the crusades to improve standards through changes to the curriculum, assessment, governance, school status, accountability, inspection, competition — and now, of course, through the national pedagogy and texts of the literacy and numeracy strategies. As Ruddock et al. (1996) observe:

> The history of reform in education . . . is of change efforts that are only partially successful because they fail to grapple with the deep structures of schooling — assumptions about what a pupil is, for instance. We would argue that one of the weaknesses of reform efforts — and we have had our fair share of them — is that they have persistently neglected an important dimension of the situation. If we are to be confident that the vast majority of young people will

commit themselves to learning . . . then we have to take seriously young people's accounts and evaluations of teaching and learning and schooling (1996: 177–8).

A number of avenues of research link the way pupils feel about themselves as learners with pupil achievement and progress. Examples of these emerge from research over recent years into:

- learning theory;
- language acquisition;
- feedback on learning;
- school effectiveness.

These four areas are very closely linked. Any messages about their inter-relationship should be given careful consideration by teachers, managers and policy makers alike. I will outline the messages from each area.

Learning theory and affective factors

The Piagetian view that children's language is structured by their developing thought processes (1969), has been modified during the last 20 years especially by Vygotsky's view of language as the tool with which a child structures concepts and understanding (1978) and with which the teacher helps scaffold the process. A point of overlap between the development of language and learning is the widely held model of learning or language acquisition as a process of active construction. We acquire new understanding when we bump into our ignorance and are forced to rearrange everything else we had previously held as knowledge, in the light of the new information. A constructivist view of language (Edwards and Mercer, 1987), where the recipient of a message is as active in building it as is the giver of the message, makes similar assumptions. It is vital therefore to manage learner attitude to *want* to build the message, if learning is to take place effectively.

A social construction model of learning is one where learners are apprentices making meaning through using language, together with the teacher and peers, to mould and manipulate concepts. The model makes specific demands in terms of learner attitude (see Figure 8.1) in that the basis of learning is 'inherently, social, cultural and communicative' (Edwards and Mercer, 1987: 168). The influences of the peer group and classroom ethos become central to the learner's engagement in the learning. If we learn through talk the learner needs:

- to feel the necessity to communicate — 'the affective foundation of thinking and learning' (Wells and Chang-Wells, 1992).

Figure 8.1:   Transmission learning/construction learning: Attitude implications

Model of learning and language	Nature of learner and teacher roles	Successful learner attitude characteristics
Transmission model	Teacher or text can transmit knowledge into learner's mind	Passivity, concentration, interest, absorption, self as reformulater, recorder, peers irrelevant
Child develops through preordained stages which modify language development (Piaget)	Provision of opportunities for child to experience discovery at first hand — learner documents, records, reflects. Child often determines pace and purpose	Practical application, acceptance, watchfulness, wonder, enquiry, concentration, willingness to learn by observation, action and error, independence, patience, tenacity, self as actor/experiencer
Child uses language to develop ideas within a 'zone of proximal development' (Vygotsky)	Teacher and learner cooperate in learning — teacher supports learner in completing task	Cooperation, trust, security, wanting to succeed, questioning, self as participant learner
Socio-construction model	Collaboration in learning with teacher and peers: defined parameters, purpose, pace and success criteria	active negotiating, self-confidence, risk-taking, peers vital, self as achiever

- to have confidence in learning in this situation maintained — 'maintaining the learner's confidence in using language as a tool for thinking with' (Sutton, 1981) — in order to take risks.
- to feel part of a peer group which values and engages in learning — what Mercer (1995) terms 'educated discourse' — exploratory, collaborative talk based in the learning task (p. 114), and dependent upon a peer group which values learning rather than regarding learning as something for boffins.

This latter point highlights again the influence of the peer group on attitudes to learning. If peer group interaction is a vital component in the construction of knowledge, then a pupil's perception of the degree to which peers value learning will impact on the learning potential for the individual within the classroom. Pollard with Filer, in their longitudinal study of young learners, conclude that they feel most positive about school when a balance is struck between the learner's allegiances to two groups: teachers and peers (1996: 309). Earlier, in a study focusing on secondary pupils Rutter concluded that 'long term educational benefits stem not from what children are specifically taught, but from the effects on children's attitudes to learning, on their self-esteem and on task orientation' (1985: 703). Pollard and Filer also observed that 'young children become effective learners when their self confidence is high, the classroom social context poses manageable risks and they receive sufficient, appropriate instruction and support' (1996: 311). The importance of affective factors on young learners is profoundly important. Separate studies (Sylva, 1994: 90; Raban-Bisby, 1995: 8) indicate that young children form early self-concepts of mastery-orientation or failure-orientation which have a major impact on later achievement or failure.

In 1996 Dr Nick Tate, the chief executive of the qualifications and Curriculum Agency (QCA) attacked the promotion of pupil self-esteem as a misguided symptom of 'moral relativism': 'Is it too heretical a thought that it is possible to place too much emphasis on self-esteem (a peculiarly late twentieth century preoccupation) and too little on some of the traditional moral qualities?' (p. 8). Can Dr Tate have made two false assumptions — first, that self-esteem is an end in itself and second, that building self-esteem and transmitting traditional morals are mutually exclusive? Surely a strong perception of the worth of the stake held by the self in learning is necessary if learners are to take on the knowledge, and values — including moral values — which schools are attempting to teach. Dr Tate ignores the self-esteem of learners at his peril — or, in fact, at theirs.

Language acquisition and affective factors

We need language in order to learn, to shunt concepts around in our mind and to manipulate emerging ideas. Acquiring language involves absorbing and constructing the language and its rules in such a way that a learner can use the language and apply it creatively in new, unrehearsed situations. One may easily substitute the words 'knowledge', 'understanding' or 'skill' for 'language' here — this view of acquisition is entirely interchangeable with such wider views of learning as those set out in National Curriculum programmes of study or advocated in OFSTED's *Framework for Inspection* (1995), both of which require children not only to take on knowledge, skills and understanding but also to use and apply their learning in new situations.

In describing the best conditions for acquiring a second language Dulay, Burt and Krashen stress the importance of the learner's willingness to take risks and the necessity for a low level of learner anxiety about the learning. The existence of a cognitive mechanism is postulated, which operates to improve language acquisition when the learner approaches learning with low anxiety and high intrinsic motivation and confidence. This 'affective filter' conversely delays language acquisition when attitudes are reversed, (1982: 51).

If primary school children's perceptions of learning play an important role in their day-to-day achievement in the classroom, if these perceptions *at a young age* are also formative in shaping subsequent achievement over many years, it follows that it is important to take such perceptions into account on a regular, systematic basis.

Feedback on learning

The way pupils feel about themselves as learners and achievers has been identified as fundamental to the process of maximizing achievement (Black and Wiliam, 1998) along with the need for pupils to feel they are making progress, to know their personal best and to be clear about the strategies for making the progress. 'What is needed is a culture of success, backed by a belief that all can achieve. Formative assessment can be a powerful weapon here if it is communicated in the right way' (p. 6). This has been established as an important issue for young learners in Key Stage 1 (Gipps and Tunstall, 1997): '. . . they understand competence and general ability; the role of the teacher and the home; the difficulty of the task; and their own behaviour: effort, speed, and interest/motivation' (p. 24). It is essential therefore that children should be viewed as sophisticated and critical learners with complex learning perceptions.

School effectiveness and affective factors

Pupil attitudes and perceptions have consistently emerged as critical factors in this field of research. Sammons, Hillman and Mortimore (1994) identified 11 factors of effective schools, one of which encompasses pupil rights and responsibilities, gathering pupil views and raising self-esteem. Coleman, Colinge and Seifert investigated the propositions that:

> student and parent attitudes to school are a function largely of the perceptions of parent and student participants of two activities: *collaboration* with students in classrooms and *willingness to communicate* with parents regarding instructional and other issues. (1993: 61)

They found that they were affected most strongly by their perceptions of the teacher as a collaborator with them in their learning and by their perceptions of the values their peers had of learning. Gray and Jesson (1990) had earlier identified affective factors as two of their three proposed measures of school performance. These were *pupil satisfaction* — the proportion of pupils in the school satisfied with the education they have received (p. 102) and *pupil–teacher relationships* — the proportion of pupils in the school who have had a good or 'vital' relationship with one or more teachers (p. 103). The third measure was academic progress.

The relationship between pupil satisfaction and achievement has been explored repeatedly over recent years (Barber, 1994; Coleman et al., 1993; FitzGibbon, 1996; Smees and Thomas, in press), but the relationship between the two has been weak. It is important, therefore, to distinguish between pupil *satisfaction* and pupil *happiness*. The attitudes I have discussed so far have been principally about confidence and motivation to learn. These do not assume

a state of happiness. In many cases, satisfied pupils may not be strongly motivated. Furthermore, I would argue that at times one can be in a not too happy
and often highly stressful state of *desperation to learn* and that the state of
desperation — when not associated with overwhelming fear of failure — can
produce significant feats of learning. It is ironic that while much of the data
systematically gathered by inspectors relates to pupils' 'attitudes to learning'
(OFSTED, 1995: 60). Many schools do not systematically gather such data for
use in self-review. One approach many schools have taken, however, is the
pupil perceptions survey.

Can pupil perception surveys capture these affective factors?

The need to find ways of systematically capturing, young pupils' perceptions
of themselves as learners is inescapable if we are to engage in improving
learning effectively at any level. By exploring perceptions we begin to see the
surface features of the attitudes beneath them.

   This research suggests that the key learning perceptions (LPs) that should
be explored are as follows:

Six Learning Perception Categories

LP1. Pupil's view of self as learner and achiever, i.e. *The pupil feels challenged, involved and successful.*

LP2. Learner's clarity about learning purpose, feedback and strategies for improvement in learning, i.e. *The pupil feels clear about own strengths and values feedback. Has a sense of how to get better.*

LP3. Pupil–teacher relationships and child's perception of teacher as collaborator in learning, i.e. *The pupil feels safe to take risks or ask for help.*

LP4. Pupil perception of parent/home support for learning and parent/school collaboration, i.e. *The pupil feels that parents value his or her work and achievement.*

LP5. Pupil perception of peer commitment to learning, i.e. *The pupil feels other pupils will value his or her achievement and work.*

LP6. Positive perception of his or her future, i.e. *The pupil feels that work now is important in the longer term and feels positive about future achievement.*

There are, of course, a number of ways of capturing perceptions. Observation,
interview and questionnaires or surveys are the most commonly used, with the
latter becoming increasingly popular in recent years. A number of surveys
have been developed and are readily available to schools or LEAs wishing to
use them. The most widely used surveys with primary aged children include
the *Pupil Survey of School Life* (Keele University, 1995), *Improving School
Effectiveness Project: Pupil Questionnaire* (MacBeath and Mortimore, 1994,
in Thomas, with McCall and Smees, 1996) and that used in the Durham
University Performance Indicators in Primary Schools System developed by
Peter Tymms at the University of Durham. A version of such a survey was also

developed as part of a school improvement project in Essex LEA. The following section offers evidence from the experience of developing and implementing a pupil perception survey within this project.

'What I think about school'

The survey 'What I think about school' was developed for use with KS1 and KS2 pupils. It is a 25-item survey which is played on tape to younger pupils in order to be accessible to those still learning to read. (The 22 questions of the survey for KS1 are also presented in a simple 'smiley' face format (see Figure 8.2). A set of the 22 questions for younger children is included at the end of this chapter. The 25 questions in the full survey are presented as a full written version for older children.)

The survey is administered by an adult unknown to the pupils. Items created from the six learning perception categories, listed in panel one above, were carefully evaluated to ensure pupils were understanding them in the way intended (see Figure 8.3).

Figure 8.2: Example item from the Year 2 survey: 'What I think about school'

1. When you get up in the morning do you look forward to going to school?

☺ Yes

☹ No

Source: Dudley, 1996

Figure 8.3: Examples of pupil explanations of the survey items

ITEMS	Pupil focus group Y2 explanation (when asked to explain the item to an imaginary pupil who does not understand)
1. When you get up in the morning, do you look forward to going to school?	This means, 'Do you like going to school?'
3. Does your teacher usually have time to listen to your questions?	'If she does then she'll listen to you — if not she won't because she's got other things to do.'
16. If children are naughty do they get told off too much *or is it fair* (the right amount)?	'. . . if they get told off the right amount.' '. . . how much they should get told off.' 'If they get told off too much they'll tell our mums and our mums'll come and have a go!'

Significantly, comparative data was provided alongside other schools so teachers could review the responses to each item by children in their school in comparison with those from children in several other schools. (Figures 8.4 and 8.5 offer illustrations from a school report showing comparative responses to survey items.)

The following issues emerged in terms of what the pupil responses indicated but also in terms of how the data were being used by schools (Dudley, 1996).

Key Stage One pupils clearly have a range of views on their learning. There are clear gender differences in pupils' perceptions at this age. On only two items did more boys respond positively than girls — indicating that slightly more boys than girls feel that they do not get stuck a lot and that their parents and teachers like each other. On many other items there are large differences — 10 per cent to 20 per cent (n = > 500) — between the sexes with boys feeling less positive than girls about access to teacher help, about how interesting work is, and about how fairly justice is administered.

Ten per cent fewer boys than girls say they read to someone at home. Interestingly 78 per cent of boys and 80 per cent of girls say they read to someone at home but only 26 per cent of girls and 22 per cent of boys responded 'Yes' to the item 'Do you read to yourself in bed or anywhere at home?'

Figure 8.4: An illustrative example of the analysis of question 4 from the survey: 'When you are at home do you sometimes think of things to tell your teacher about?'

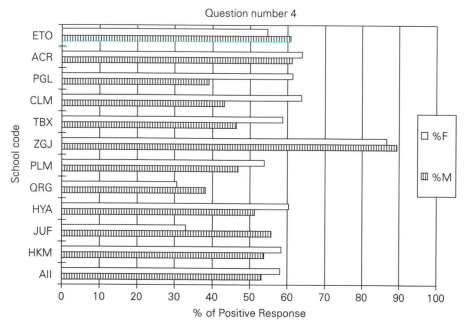

Figure 8.5: Analysis of question 20 to indicate differences in response between boys and girls: 'When your teacher shows your work to the class do you worry about what people will say to you afterwards?'

Replies were given on a four point scale from (1) **never** to (2) **sometimes** to (3) **quite often** to (4) **always.**

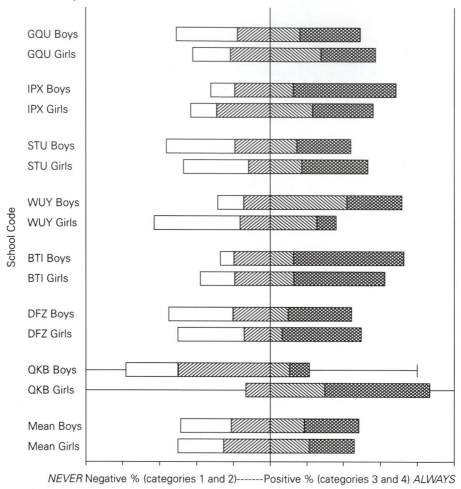

NEVER Negative % (categories 1 and 2)-------Positive % (categories 3 and 4) *ALWAYS*
Percentage Response

How effective is the survey in capturing learning perceptions?

The items are prescribed and the responses are closed, reducing the power of the survey to generate discussion at school beyond responding to the bare statistics. However, the following points did emerge as important outcomes of using the survey. It raised some debates among teachers about children's responses to the items. Some of this debate ended in positive suggestions for further enquiry into the issues behind the pupil responses; possible decisions to improve pupil attitudes to learning; improving opportunities for learning.

The strengths of the learning perception survey in generating initial discussion focusing positively on enquiry and change have been a result of:

- the potential the survey has for generating comparative data which led to positive action focused discussion and allowed strategies for change;
- the fact that feedback is given against the actual survey items rather than against more abstract 'categories';
- the fact that it allows for a 100 per cent sample of pupils;
- the fact that it allows for examination of the responses separately by gender.

Limitations and weaknesses are shared with other closed-item survey approaches. The items do not necessarily reflect the issues or situation of the individual school or pupils. Where teachers criticized the methodology it was often in relation to the wording of items or the possibility that children were interpreting them in different ways or did not understand the item. There was a frustration in some discussion about the need to get to the individual pupil responses. There was also however, an acceptance of the majority of the issues behind the data.

Do pupil perceptions count?

In dealing with perceptions it is important to remember that what counts is how pupils feel — not whether they have any justification for the feeling. Sometimes, where learning perception data were rejected, it was as result of a reluctance by teachers to give credence to pupils' feelings as expressed through the survey. For instance, the item 'Do your parents and your teacher like each other?' was rejected on one occasion on the basis of the view: 'Because I don't think they know . . . so it's really based very much on the child's feelings isn't it.'

There was a confusion about what the data represent — not objective facts about parent/teacher relations but a 'gut feeling' from the child. Certainly there is a need to understand that perceptions are purely 'perceptions' but we need to learn to act on the basis that they are real even if we may disagree with them. In the main the issues behind the responses were accepted. One school which had given pupils' perception questionnaires before had developed a clearer understanding of the nature of pupil feelings and perceptions:

- 'I mean issues come up that we take exception to but it's obviously their perception.'
- 'And I don't think they're clever enough to fix it to please us do you?'

This, however, argues for *school generated* items. There was the potential in this survey for schools to add their own items although none did. It also argues for a greater use of open items. Much more work needs to be done on accessing all children to more open items; this has been shown to be a powerful means of capturing learning perceptions (Cooper and MacIntyre, 1995; MacBeath, 1996; Scottish Office Education Department, 1992). This increases administration time and does not produce easily used comparative data. It is, therefore, likely that discussion and analysis of open items will need to be taken up at school level as part of the follow-up to the survey. Pupil interviews may be a more potent and useful strategy of gathering data on a regular basis. One reason for using a survey is for a periodic review of pupil attitudes in comparison with those from a range of other — perhaps similar schools — but often this is not sufficiently specific to be good diagnostic data. It has led one school to add to their list of management check points following any agreed policy change not only: 'How will this be viewed by the staff and by parents?' but also now 'How will it be perceived by pupils?'

Comparative data

The availability of comparative data from other schools is a key trigger to this process. It enables teachers to answer the question — 'How would pupils in another [similar] school respond to this item?' Reaction to the comparative aspect of the survey was very positive. This is illustrated in one headteacher's comments after comparing her own pupil's responses to the item 'Does your teacher have time to listen to your questions?' with those of pupils in other similar schools. She noticed a big difference and said, later, 'I was worried about that — I actually talked to the staff about that. Are we passing on our pressurization to the pupils?'

Discussions at the school subsequently led to a classroom inquiry by the teachers into how they respond to pupils when they feel under pressure of numbers and time. Another responded to the survey: '. . . well it makes you think "What am I doing? Am I not being fair? And how am I not being fair?"'

There was also acceptance that improving pupil understanding of classroom strategies could produce a changed pupil perception: 'You can actually influence the way they think, the way they understand . . . so they may answer that question quite differently if they understood [teacher strategies] better.'

Many have suggested adapting the survey for use as a more open tool for classroom evaluation. 'It will be nice to follow it up knowing the children because you can actually piece things together — a picture of the child and their perceptions.'

Developing alternative more open approaches to gathering pupil perception data is an important area of further investigation and development if schools are to make further enquiry into pupil perception issues. 'I can see it being useful for the children at the end of term or whatever as a way of sort of self assessing themselves . . . some of the questions are quite useful to have discussions with the children about aren't they?'

It is vital that educators accept that young pupils have perceptions and feelings which are as legitimate and important to consider in that they affect their predisposition to learn. It is not for adults to decide how real or objective they are, but rather to observe, measure and research how they may be harnessed in promoting learning. It is also vital for LEAs and school improvement projects or education action zones to develop a capacity to capture and analyse these perceptions with schools as part of a systematic set of pupil data considered in the process of determining school improvement and target setting. Pupil perception data is a powerful trigger for reflection and change. It needs to become a source of information which is revisited in the process of monitoring improvement and not be cast aside once the need for change has been established.

Current research-in-process being carried out into the Improving School Effectiveness Project (ISEP) Pupil Questionnaire (MacBeath and Mortimore, 1994) indicates that the items relating to the *learner's engagement with school* and *self-esteem as a learner* are those being investigated as the categories with the greatest potential for use as what Smees and Thomas term 'separate dimensions of pupil performance' (Smees and Thomas, 1998: 10).

> in terms of identifying the kinds of affective outcomes that may be developed for the purpose of providing comparative feedback to schools, 'self-esteem' and 'engagement with school' are two areas that may prove fruitful. (Thomas with McCall and Smees, 1996: 8)

This survey approach to exploring pupil perceptions of learning can, thus, play a part in building pupil perceptions into the information and decision-making processes which schools use in planning for development and improvement. The DfEE is to legislate for publication by schools of annual improvement targets (DfEE, 1997). If cognitive gains are dependent on affective and metacognitive factors then it is clear that targets which focus on improved test scores alone will not provide schools with any measure of the factors which are increasing pupil's capacity to learn or of their motivation and commitment to learning. Corbett and Southworth give this warning

> with a narrow range of aspects assessed it is likely that only targets for improvement related to published national data will be given public validity, then improvement across other curricular aims may be considered unimportant. (1996: 11)

One could go a step further and suggest that if improvement in metacognition and affective factors are not considered alongside learning outcome measures,

Figure 8.6: The triangular relationships between targets in pupil learning and the effects of the perceptions of pupils, parents, peers and teachers

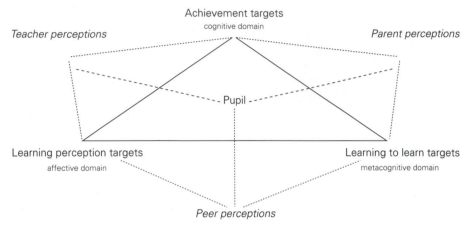

then the impact on children's later cognitive achievement will be negative in the medium and longer term.

These 'other curricular aims' are vital to measure and consider in plans for school improvement and enhanced learning. Figure 8.6 provides an illustration of how pupil learning can be viewed at the centre of a web of teacher, parental and peer perceptions in the identification of achievement targets. Smees and Thomas argue that the ISEP survey data: 'should be combined with other information available within school to stimulate an ongoing discussion of ways to target areas for improvement' (1998: 11).

Ideally, then, school targets for pupil achievement should be accompanied by 'learning targets' (Essex County Council, 1997) reflecting these other 'curricular aims' or 'curriculum targets' (DfEE, 1998) which may well address issues such as improving boys' attitudes to reading in upper KS2 or increasing the frequency with which KS1 pupils read to themselves at home.

Pupils as data gatherers and researchers

One way of developing the use of pupil data is to involve the pupils as participant researchers in data gathering and analysis (Fielding, 1998). Work now needs to be done in order to develop ways of combining pupil-led research with learning perception data survey outcomes. This can greatly increase the validity and the potential for practical use of such surveys. There are important questions to ask before pupils are involved in this. These include those listed as follows:

Questions to ask before involving pupils as researchers:

- When we are attempting to gain a pupil perspective on an issue within school, who devises and asks the questions?
- When we ask pupils to carry out research are we asking them to research 'real' issues which will make a difference to their life in school?
- Have we trained pupils in aspects of data gathering or research? Do they feel equal participants? Do we have an agreed protocol about the status and use of pupil research data? Are parents comfortable with and informed about the processes?
- Can we and do we use pupil self assessments, evaluations of teaching, or contributions to annual reports in any systematic way? Do we involve pupils in the process of analysing and reporting? Are pupil perceptions used systematically in identifying improvement or development planning priorities? Do pupils or does the school council report to governors or other bodies?
- When we involve pupils as researchers either formally or informally, do we share with them the outcomes of the research?

Words of warning
Pupil perceptions can be eye-opening and supportive but they can also be bruising. Are you ready for what their research data might bring? Are you going to give it the weight it deserves or are you going to deny the data that does not fit your perceptions? How will you resolve such dilemmas?

Pupils' perception surveys and policy makers

In 1994 Michael Barber wrote, '. . . if more teachers are to succeed in unlocking the potential of young people in adolescence, then issues of attitude, motivation, pupil self-esteem and peer group culture must take centre stage' (Barber, 1994: 5). Four years later the Campaign for Learning, supported by the DfEE, published a MORI survey of secondary school pupils' attitudes to learning. The results made front page news in the *Times Educational Supplement* (TES, 1998). The survey reflected many of the findings of previous surveys, but what is interesting is the involvement of the DfEE — in which Professor Barber heads the Standards and Effectiveness Unit — in supporting such a survey. This is the first time the government has become so closely involved in surveying pupil perceptions. In the main this should be welcomed as representing a step forward for the UK government in moving towards implementing the 1989 UN Convention on the Rights of the Child, Article 12 of which states that every child who is capable of forming his or her own views must have the right to 'express those views freely in all matters affecting the child'. The potential for pupil views to become another political football must also be treated with caution. Madden has warned that, 'the motivation of those who commission attitude surveys among the young has to be considered as well as the methodologies used in constructing the questions and analysing the responses' (1996: 20). She goes on to add, however, that 'combining questionnaire data with the outcomes of more customised, sensitive probings from carefully constructed discussion can provide hugely illuminating intelligence about young people' (1996: 20).

Perhaps what is really needed in the future is the inclusion on every OFSTED inspection team not only of the current registered inspector, team inspectors and lay inspector but also of a *pupil* inspector — trained and accredited by OFSTED. Working closely to the framework, the pupil inspector would observe lessons, interview pupils and staff and make judgments which would inform the final report. A crazy idea maybe — but ask a few pupils. They may say it might just work!

Items included in the Y2 Learning Perception Survey: What I think about School

(The main purpose of the survey is to promote discussion about pupil perceptions of learning and to raise questions or issues that can be investigated further. It is not intended to give answers. The survey is designed to elicit responses to six areas of pupil perception which research indicates influences pupil achievement. These include the following: the child's view of self as a learner and achiever; the learner's clarity about learning purpose, feedback and strategies for improvement in learning; teacher/pupil relationships and pupil perceptions of the teacher as a collaborator in learning; pupil perceptions of parent/home support for learning and parent/school collaboration; pupil perceptions of peer commitment to learning; and perceptions of future learning and achievement.)

1   When you get up in the morning do you look forward to going to school?
2   Are the children in the school nice to smaller children (about their work)?
3   Does your teacher usually have time to listen to your questions?
4   When you are at home do you sometimes think of things to tell your teacher about?
5   When you are at home do you talk about things you have been doing at school?
6   Do you read to someone at home?
7   Do you read to yourself in bed (or anywhere at home)?
8   What sort of work are you good at? Is it . . . or nothing?
9   Do your parents come to the school and talk to your teacher?
10   Do your parents and your teacher like each other?
11   When you have finished your work at school, do you usually know what you have to do next?
12   Is the work usually boring or interesting?
13   Have you ever done some work your teacher thought was really good?
14   When you need help, does your teacher help you?
15   Is a lot of the work too easy for you?

16 When your teacher looks at your work, how do you feel?

17 When children are naughty are the teachers fair — Do the children get told off too much or the right amount?

18 Do you get stuck a lot?

19 Are the grown-ups in the school nice to you?

20 When your teacher shows your work to the class do you worry about what people will say about it afterwards?

21 Do you think you are going to be good at school work when you are older?

22 People say that what you learn at school is important for when you are grown up. Do you think this is true?

References

BARBER, M. (1994) *Young People and Their Attitudes to School: An Interim Report of a Research Project in the Centre for Successful Schools*, Keele: University of Keele.

BLACK, P. and WILIAM, D. (1998) *Assessment and Classroom Learning*, London: School of Education, Kings College, University of London.

COLEMAN, P., COLLINGE, J. and SEIFERT, I. (1993) 'Seeking the levers of change: Participant attitudes and school improvement', in *School Effectiveness and School Improvement*, **4**, (1), 59–83.

COOPER, P. and MACINTYRE, D. (1995) 'The crafts of the classroom: Teachers' and students' accounts of the knowledge underpinning effective teaching and learning in classrooms', *Research Papers in Education* **10**, (2), London: Routledge, pp. 181–216.

CORBETT, F. and SOUTHWORTH, G. (1996) 'Improving primary schools: Insights and ideas from the first year of the Essex Primary School Improvement and Research and Development Programme'. Unpublished paper prepared for BERA September 1996 Annual Conference, Lancaster University.

DfEE (1997) *From Targets to Action: Guidance to Support Effective Target Setting in Schools*, London: Department for Education and Employment.

DfEE (1998) 'Introduction of the national literacy strategy to LEAs', Notes for conference delegates, Appendix 9 Blank School Target Setting proforma.

DUDLEY, P. (1996) 'What I think about school, learning perception survey for year two and year four pupils', Unpublished.

DULAY, H., BURT, M. and KRASHEN, S. (1982) *Language Two*, Oxford: Oxford University Press.

EDWARDS, D. and MERCER, N. (1987) *Common Knowledge. The Development of Understanding in the Classroom*, London: Methuen.

ESSEX COUNTY COUNCIL, LEARNING SERVICES DIRECTORATE (1997) *Setting and Achieving Challenging Target*, Chelmsford: Essex Advisory and Inspection Services.

FIELDING, M. (1998) 'Students as researchers: From data source to significant voice', Paper presented to the 11th International Congress for School Effectiveness and Improvement, Manchester: University of Manchester School of Education, 4–7 January.

FITZ-GIBBON, C.T. (1996) *Monitoring Education*, London: Cassell.

GIPPS, C. and TUNSTALL, P. (1997) 'Effort, ability and the teacher: Young children's explanations for success and failure', Paper presented at the annual conference of the British Educational Research Association, York: University of York, September.

GRAY, J. and JESSON, D. (1990) 'The negotiation and construction of performance indicators: Some principles, proposals and problems', *Evaluation and Research in Education*, **4**, (2), pp. 93–108.

KEELE UNIVERSITY (1994) *Pupil Survey of School Life*, Centre for Successful Schools, Keele: Keele University.

MACBEATH, J., BOYD, B., RAND, J. and BELL, S. (1996) *Schools Speak for Themselves: Towards a Framework for School Self-evaluation*, London: NUT.

MACBEATH, J. and MORTIMORE, P. (1994) *Improving School Effectiveness Project: Pupil Questionnaire*, Edinburgh: Scottish Office Education Department.

MADDEN, M. (1996) 'How to hype up adult alarm with surveys of the young', in *The Times Educational Supplement*, 24 May 1996, p. 20.

MERCER, D. (1995) *The Guided Construction of Knowledge*, London: Multilingual Matters.

MORTIMORE, P., SAMMONS, P., STOLL, L., LEWIS, D. and ECOB, R. (1988) *School Matters: The Junior Years*, London: Paul Chapman Publishing.

OFSTED (1995) *Framework for the Inspection of Primary Schools*, Office for Standards in Education, London: HMSO.

PIAGET, J. (1969) *The Language and Thought of the Child*, London: Routledge.

POLLARD, A. with FILER, A. (1996) *The Social World of Children's Learning*, London: Cassell.

'Pupils give voice to their criticisms', *Times Educational Supplement*, 15-5–98, p. 1.

RABAN-BISBY, B. (1995) *Early Childhood Years — Problem or Resource?* Dean's Lecture Series 1995, Melbourne, Australia: The University of Melbourne.

RUDDOCK, J., CHAPLIN, R. and WALLACE, G. (eds) (1996) *School Improvement: What Can the Pupils Tell Us?*, London: Fulton.

RUTTER, M. (1985) 'Family and social influences on cognitive development', *Journal of Child Psychology*, **26**, (5), pp. 683–704.

SAMMONS, P. (1993) *The Continuity of School Effect*, London: University of London Institute of Education.

SAMMONS, P., HILLMAN, J. and MORTIMORE, P. (1994) *Key Characteristics of Effective Schools: A Review of School Effectiveness Research*, London: Office for Standards in Education (OFSTED).

SCOTTISH OFFICE EDUCATION DEPARTMENT (1992) *Using Ethos Indicators in Primary School Self Evaluation*, Edinburgh: HMSO.

SMEES, R. and THOMAS, S. (in press) 'Valuing pupils' views about school'. ISEIC, *British Journal of Curriculum and Assessment*, London: University of London Institute of Education.

SUTTON, C. (1981) *Communicating in the Classroom*, London: Hodder and Stoughton.

SYLVA, K. (1994) 'The impact of early learning on children's later development' (4.1) in BALL, C. (ed.) *Start Right: The Importance of Early Learning*, London: Royal Society of Arts.

THOMAS, S., with MCCALL, J. and SMEES, R. (1996) 'Room for improvement: Analysis of primary baseline measures', Paper presented at the annual conference of the British Educational Research Association, Lancaster.

WELLS, G. and CHANG-WELLS, G. (1992) *Constructing Knowledge Together: Classrooms as Centres of Enquiry and Literacy*, London: Heinemann.

9   Value-added Assessment

Colin Conner

With increasing demands throughout the world for improved efficiency and standards from education systems (Harris, Keys and Fernandes, 1997; Reynolds and Farrell, 1996), there has been extensive effort invested in developing ways of monitoring effectiveness. As Goldstein and Woodhouse (1996) have argued, 'Since the principal aim of educational institutions is to promote learning it would appear natural to evaluate their accomplishment of this aim by comparing the performances of students who attend them' (1996: 135). Broadfoot (1996) recognizes the power of such comparative evaluations. Not only can the results be used to identify strengths and weaknesses of individuals, institutions and whole systems, results can also be used as a powerful source of leverage to bring about change. As she suggests, 'It is for this reason that we are increasingly seeing policy makers in many countries quite deliberately manipulating assessment policies in order to alter priorities of the educational system with a view to improving effectiveness' (1996: 21).

A strategy that has been the subject of increasing interest is the concept of 'value added', the potential policy implications of which were recognized by the former Secretary of State, Gillian Shephard, who commented, 'I am firmly committed to the development of robust national measures of value-added by schools . . . Published alongside National Curriculum assessments and the results of public examinations, such measures have the capacity to enrich the available information about the effectiveness of schools . . .' (Shephard, 1994).

Birnbaum defines value added as an attempt,

> . . . to estimate the influence of the school by comparing the achievements of its pupils in relation to a number of factors, the most important of which is the student's prior ability. In order to assess the influence of schools on achievement, the best approaches to value added look at the relationship between prior ability and achievement for each individual pupil. (DfE: 1995)

Further clarification of the concept of value added is offered in a briefing paper produced by the Department for Education (DfE) which described the term value added in education as shorthand for what schools and colleges add to their pupils' and students' knowledge, skills and understanding between one age and another. The object of trying to develop ways of measuring it is to allow us to 'compare the changes in attainment over time of pupils or students in a particular school or college with those of the wider student population' (1995: 1).

In the DfE publication it is argued that if reliable and consistent measures can be devised, they can provide useful information about the contribution which schools and colleges themselves have made towards the results achieved by their pupils and students. It is also suggested that measures of value added at the *national level* are needed to enable the performance of schools and colleges to be compared consistently across the country.

Value-added measures can also be used at the *local level* to help school and college managers plan and target resources more effectively. Local measures of value added can be more detailed than those designed for national application, and so can help to identify differences in performance within a single institution or between a group of local institutions using the same measures.

A direct result of this has been increasing emphasis on the development of baseline assessment processes (see Fisher, 1995, and Wolfendale, 1993, for useful reviews) in order that children's progress can be charted from nursery to infant, from infant to junior and from junior to secondary. In the process, it is assumed, the effectiveness of teachers and the education system can be more clearly monitored. Mary Jane Drummond provides an important note of caution about such initiatives, in particular, that there is, 'an overwhelming tendency to measure not what is of most value, but what is easily measured' (1992: 67).

Value added was a topic that exercised the thinking of the National Commission on Education in their publication 'Learning to succeed' (1993), where they argued that in considering the effectiveness of the educational system, 'Information should always be included which enables the value of the contribution of schools themselves to be judged' (NCE 1993: 66).

To advise them they invited Professor Andrew McPherson of the University of Edinburgh to produce a briefing paper on value added (McPherson, 1993). The briefing paper opens with probably the most fundamental question concerning value added and asks, *does value added information allow us to say that one school is necessarily better than another or better or worse than it used to be?* McPherson also goes on to question how information can be used and not abused, and how we can be sure that it will meet the needs of all who might wish to use it. He identifies a number of central issues that should be considered when using value-added information.

- School's test and examination results are informative, but raw results are misleading indicators of the added value of a school if they are not also adjusted for intake differences. Schools and their context differ from one another and these differences significantly influence progress and achievement. Whereas raw results tell us about absolute standards of attainment, offer a means of monitoring attainment across the country as a whole and for identifying low levels of attainment by some groups, they say little about how well the school that children have attended has contributed to their success. 'In contrast, by controlling for the effects of pupils' abilities or prior attainment, value-added analyses allow more precise identification of schools where factors such as school management and the quality of teaching have contributed to pupils' success' (Strand, 1998: 135).

- Raw results should therefore be accompanied by an assessment of the contribution a school makes to its pupils' progress. The assessment should take account of each pupil's prior level of attainment and of other factors inside and outside the school that may have influenced progress.
- A single statistic may not adequately summarize progress. Different types of pupil progress at different rates and some progress is correlated with factors outside of the teacher's control. These include:

> household size and adult composition; the educational level of the parent or parents; and the parents' occupations. Other factors associated with progress include the level of material and social (dis)advantage in the immediate neighbourhood of the home and aspects of the wider opportunity structure, including the level and character of local employment opportunities, and the opportunities for further progress in education and training. (McPherson, 1993: 6)

McPherson suggests that what is needed is a good indicator system which:

- takes account of different needs and uses of value-added information;
- is as simple as possible, while accounting for different individualities (i.e. pupils, families, schools and communities);
- employs a variety of measures that provide stable illustrations of the reality of pupils' progress rather than 'single snapshots of performance';
- employs means of monitoring and improving its own validity.

A clear explanation of the implications of this for the primary school is provided in a pamphlet produced by the School Curriculum and Assessment Authority (SCAA) in collaboration with the Centre for the study of Comprehensive Schools (CSCS). The pamphlet defines value added as, '. . . a way of measuring the progress made by pupils from one Key Stage to the next, relative to the progress made by other similar pupils' (1996: 6).

In order to produce reliable value-added measures, it is argued that schools will need to have available the results of the same pupils at both the beginning (input) and at the end (outcome) of the process. SCAA warns against placing too much reliance on measures where there is a small number of pupils, or where pupil turnover is high. (Interestingly, there is no formal recognition that the continual changes to the curriculum may lead to discrepancies in comparison from one key stage to the next. Strand (1998) also reminds us that the effect of the teacher boycott of National Curriculum assessment in 1993 and 1994 means that a proper illustration of the value added from Key Stage 1 to Key Stage 2 will not really be available until 1999 at the earliest). Calculations of value added are normally presented in terms of a 'regression line', or 'line of

Figure 9.1: Two examples of value-added analysis

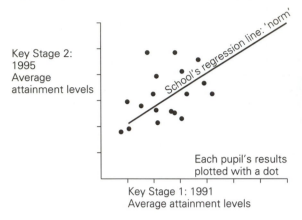

Key Stage 2:
1995
Average
attainment levels

Each pupil's progress is plotted on the graph. Those above the line have made better than expected progress. Those below the line have made less progress than expected.

Each pupil's results
plotted with a dot

Key Stage 1: 1991
Average attainment levels

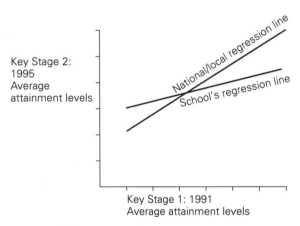

Key Stage 2:
1995
Average
attainment levels

The school regression line shows that pupils with lower attainment at 7 years of age have progressed better on average than similar pupils nationally, while pupils with higher attainment at 7 have progressed less well.

Key Stage 1: 1991
Average attainment levels

Source: SCAA/CSCS 1996

best fit'. These show the average progress made by pupils from one starting point to another. Figure 9.1 presents two examples of value-added analysis from Key Stage 1 to Key Stage 2. The first compares individual pupils against the school's average added value and the second compares the school with the national picture.

The SCAA/CSCS pamphlet suggests that the data should be considered in relation to the questions it asks of the school. For example, what has caused the school to be more effective with one group than another and what action might be needed?

The Society of Education Officers (1996) in their consideration of value added in education also suggest that such analyses may contribute to answering important questions related to school improvement. 'Value-added analyses provide underpinning evidence as part of the much wider range of information and stimuli which schools receive. The evidence allows schools to make better informed decisions about how to effect higher achievement throughout the school' (1996: 7).

An example of such analyses for a primary school in relation to clearly identified questions can be seen in an article by Mangan (1997), who explains that in his school, the process of collecting data on pupil performance transcends the school year and includes a range of evidence gathering procedures including teacher observation, the county baseline assessment materials, end of Key Stage Assessments and the Performance Indicators in Primary Schools Project (PIPS). The PIPS Project is based at the Universities of Newcastle and Durham and is described as 'a confidential, measurement based, self assessment tool for self-evaluation'. A timetable of assessments is provided for the academic year which requires participating schools to administer standardized tests to pupils in the reception class and in Years 2, 3, 4, and 6 at a given time and to return the unmarked scripts to the project team for marking. They then plot the progress made by pupils in each of the assessed areas and comparison of the relative rates of progress of pupils in participating schools with those from all of the other schools in the project. (In 1997 when the article was written, there were 1507 schools and 141,466 primary aged pupils in the project. Code names are used to protect the identity of each school, but it is possible to contact schools with similar contexts who appear to be making greater progress.)

Assessments are undertaken of children's performance in reading, maths and science as well as a picture vocabulary test, a non-verbal ability test and a measure of home background. Where children have scored higher on a test, or made greater progress than original scores indicated was likely, schools are seen to have added value to these pupils. If the majority of pupils have achieved over and above their suggested potential, then these schools might be seen as being successful schools.

Mangan explains that when his school received the first illustration of the analysis of its results from PIPs team, the presentation of the findings to the staff generated a great deal of staff discussion and potential explanations were considered. Some highlighted the need for further investigation and others for immediate action, for example,

- Several pupils were identified as making less progress than expected, some of whom were previously unidentified. The resulting discussion led the staff to question why this might be so, whether there was a need to demand more of these pupils or whether the school was failing to motivate them sufficiently? (Each teacher agreed to examine existing practice to seek further explanations and report back.)
- Pupils in some classes seemed to be making better progress in reading and science than in mathematics. Again this caused the staff to question why this had happened. Was it the result of a recent focus on reading for example? (Subject coordinators were invited to monitor the situation more closely with a view to reporting back to the senior management team.)

- The evidence also indicated that the girls were usually out-performing the boys in reading and mathematics but not in science. This resulted in the teachers questioning whether they were doing enough to help boys reach their potential? Similarly they asked whether they were doing enough to promote science with the girls? (Subject coordinators agreed to consult with advisory staff for advice and class teachers agreed to monitor the ways in which boys are encouraged).

Mangan concluded that,

> Early indications are that this process is proving to be particularly valuable in helping us to consider possible developmental targets for each cohort, for individual members of staff and for the school as a whole. It would appear therefore that when armed with more of this kind of information in the future, our school curriculum and development plans will become increasingly focused upon meeting the children's needs and upon improving pupil performance across the school. (1997: 17)

Another illustration of the way in which primary schools are responding to value-added analyses can be seen in an article by Jackie Pfister (1997) who suggests that looking at her own school's evidence opened her eyes about her school's performance. She divides her school's value-added analysis into two groups, 'Little value added' and 'Big value added'.

'Little value added' relates to the information which derives from National Curriculum assessment results. It is described in this way because it constitutes a relatively small part of the evaluation evidence that a school gathers during the course of a school year. It is important, however, because it places school evaluation in a broader national context and provides standardized evidence against which to compare the school's progress. However, despite its importance, not least to target setting, the amount of feedback it can give is regarded as limited. Analysing progress against national and county averages is useful but she warns against jumping to conclusions too quickly, and argues for careful reflection,

> We . . . weigh up our observations, together with other evidence, with both critical caution and respect. Unless our deliberations result in positive action, the pay-off is not worth the time spent. Action could mean reviewing, acknowledging, communicating or simply congratulating. (1997: 23)

'Big value added', on the other hand, is concerned with broader school outcomes and ranges across the curriculum and the effectiveness of its implementation, to areas of school management and to the strengths and weaknesses of the pastoral arrangements in the school. As Mangan's article illustrated, questions serve as a useful focus for deliberations; How effectively have we created channels to foster shared understandings with parents and pupils? Are things being accomplished at home and at school in practice as well as in policy? Are we seeing the progress and standards that demonstrate improvement?

Pfister argues that the data and evidence that these processes accumulate are useless in isolation and require 'the corporate wisdom and good will of the teachers to contextualise, interpret and identify actions which should arise' (1997: 25). For this to be effective she suggests that an honest, reflective and non-defensive approach to new information and data analysis is vital, 'I take the view that team issues are shared with the team and any individual issues with the individual' (1997: 25). She accepts that initially her analysis was rather crude, but that with experience she and her colleagues are able to distinguish between issues that are worth pursuing and those that are irrelevant or unimportant at this particular moment.

> But as we continue to expand this picture of our work by means of both quantitative and qualitative evidence, the webbing between the two — the interaction between the specific and the contextual — creates meaning and understanding that becomes less crude incrementally. Where numerical data is relevant and useful — and it often is — we use it . . . it allows us to value what we do well in a slightly sharper and more evidenced way. (1997: 25)

An evaluation of the reactions of primary schools to value-added activities was investigated in a small scale project undertaken for Hertfordshire by Conner and Southworth (1997). A sample of seven schools was included in the evaluation to reflect a range of school size, school context and experience of value-added analyses. Each school was visited twice and prior to each visit a common set of questions was used to enquire into each school's approach. The first visit explored the following questions;

- What does the term value added mean to you?
- Why do you think it is important?
- How is it organized in your school?
- How is value-added information used?
- Who has access to the information?
- In the light of experience so far, what do you regard as the benefits and weaknesses of using such an approach?

The second visit focused on the following questions;

- Since the last visit what has happened about value added in your school?
- Have any staff been involved in using value-added analyses of the schools's performance?
- How do you envisage value-added analyses developing?
- What plans do you have for baseline assessment?
- What are your reactions to the proposals for target setting?
- How do you see target setting relating to your value-added work?

The findings of the project have to be regarded as interim because the work was suspended at an earlier stage than was originally intended, but some interesting findings emerged with regard to reactions to the issues involved. The main findings are summarized below:

1   There were a wide ranging set of interpretations of the term 'value added', from a strictly quantitative interpretation based on the analysis of National Curriculum results to a recognition that it related to the value of all that went on in the school.

2   At the time of the investigation, each of the schools was using different approaches and were at different stages of developing value-added analyses of their performance.

3   The participating schools emphasized the need to take account of pupil's social development as well as their academic progress. Concern was also expressed that the measures that were used to make comparisons were open to question. There have been so many changes to the curriculum and its assessment procedures that there is uncertainty about whether we are comparing like with like. If this is true, how confident can we be that we are really measuring progress from one stage to another and the value that is being added?

4   In some of the schools only the headteachers were involved in analysing assessment information for value-added purposes. In others, deputies and teachers were involved, usually the assessment coordinator.

5   The most effective approaches were in contexts where teachers were given responsibility for considering the implications of assessment data for children in their classes.

6   There was evidence in some schools that target setting was taking place. (This was before there was a government requirement for this to occur.)

7   In schools which were developing target setting, baseline information was being collected and teachers were being asked to predict pupils' levels of achievement at the end of key stages. For example, teachers of Y1 classes in one school were predicting children's levels at the end of Key Stage 1.

8   A number of important management issues emerged:

    •   The first relates to the skills of analysis. We were made aware by most headteachers that they needed help in this area.
    •   Those heads who had begun to 'grapple with the information' still felt that they were in an early stage of learning and were uncertain about which information it was necessary to focus upon.
    •   The process needs to be managed. At present, most headteachers are still examining when it is most appropriate within the school year to conduct the monitoring, collection and

analysis of pupil data. When it is the best time to do these tasks in relation to the rhythms of the school year remains unclear.

- Finding the time to analyse was also seen as being difficult and the fear that excessive analysis may be unnecessary. Some felt that the time invested in the analyses was not always rewarded with significant outcomes. Others said that all the analysis achieved was confirmation of existing knowledge. There was also the fact that sometimes a lot of time was devoted to examining the information associated with relatively small numbers of pupils.
- Another important management issue was related to the allocation of responsibilities. One of the schools was beginning to consider how to deploy subject managers so that they played an integral part in undertaking value-added analyses as part of their monitoring responsibilities.
- There was evidence in some schools of coordination and management of the process by groups of staff who would have responsibility for setting targets and the management of assessment information for their group of classes, which were often divided by age or stage. One headteacher argued that it was important to develop a stronger sense of responsibility across the key stage teams of teachers for the end of key stage achievements and not assume that this was the responsibility solely of the Y2 or Y6 teacher.
- There were some instances where changes in staffing during the project created difficulties for sustaining progress and commitment and continuity in the value-added activities. When key players in developing an evidence based approach leave a school, developments can be adversely affected unless systems are established that everyone understands and apply consistently.

9   An important point made by all of the headteachers was the assumption that a school will always add more and more value year on year. We were reminded by the headteachers that there are situations where, however much effort is put into particular year groups, the composition of the year group will influence overall achievements and lead to the assessment results showing no improvement against previous years. In fact, it could be the case that with some cohorts there could be regression.

10   There were clear benefits to adopting a value-added approach. There was evidence that pupil progress and improved achievements were attributed to the focus that value-added analysis had provided. We were also told on a number of occasions that the process of analysing

pupil data made staff question their assumptions and expectations for pupils. The prediction of anticipated levels of achievement based upon the analysis of data seemed to be concentrating minds. As a result, the headteachers in the survey felt there was a greater attention being paid to pupils' learning outcomes.

Conclusion

Whereas the advocates of value-added analyses see nothing but good emerging from the deliberations presented here, there are limitations, since all the evidence suggests that, 'The main substantive conclusion to be drawn from the analyses that have been conducted to date is that the considerable majority of schools achieve precisely the sort of results one would predict from knowledge of their intake' (Gray, 1996: 128).

Gray also adds that the majority of efforts to establish data bases at the pre-school, early years and primary stages has not been particularly successful so far and that in evaluating any institution it is clear that contextualization is fundamentally important.

> By this we mean the taking account of factors which influence outcome measures and over which the institution has little control . . . In other words, schools and institutions in general should be held accountable for the things they can be expected to influence, rather than for the characteristics the student brings with them when they enter. This principle should underpin attempts to devise methods of value added against which to judge schools. (Gray, 1996: 131)

In support of this, Gray believes that there should be three core assumptions underpinning any value-added activities;

- schools should be compared on a like with like basis;
- the progress of pupils from their respective starting points should be the prime concern;
- educational institutions vary in their effectiveness in boosting their pupils' progress for a variety of justifiable reasons.

It is also important to remember that the suggestions presented here relate only to a part of what schools are about. As Goldstein has recently suggested, 'When discussing the use of test or examination results, remember that educational institutions have a responsibility for encouraging children's learning and development across a much wider range of areas than reasonably can be tested by school league tables' (Goldstein, 1997: 18).

A similar conclusion is offered by Mary Jane Drummond in Chapter 2, when she emphasizes that the most effective schools do more than add value to children's levels of attainment as measured by test scores. In effective schools, 'children listen to music, meet artists in residence, visit the sea, climb hills, look down microscopes and much more'.

It is clear, however, that gathering appropriate information together does help schools draw more sensible and sensitive conclusions about their practice and their children's achievements and by implication to identify reasonable and realistic targets for school improvement which go beyond those just related to academic gains.

Note

This is an extended version of an article that appeared in *Primary File*, **31**, 1998.

References

BIRNBAUM, I. (1993) 'Value added variations', *Education*, **18**, (20).

BROADFOOT, P. (1996) 'Assessment and learning: Power or partnership', Ch. 3 in GOLDSTEIN, H. and LEWIS, T. (eds), *Assessment: Problems, Developments and Statistical Issues*, Chichester: John Wiley.

CONNER, C. and SOUTHWORTH, G. (1997) 'An evaluation of approaches to value-added work in Hertfordshire Primary Schools', Interim report, unpublished paper, Cambridge: University of Cambridge School of Education.

DfE (1995) 'Value added in education: A briefing paper from the Department for Education', London: HMSO.

DRUMMOND, M.J. (1992) 'Assessing learning in the early years', *Forum*, **34**, (3), pp. 66–8.

FISHER, D. (1995) *Baseline Assessment*, Education Management Information Exchange Snapshort, Slough: NFER.

GOLDSTEIN, H. (1997) 'Value added tables: The less-than-the holy grail', *Managing Schools Today*, **6**, (6), March.

GOLDSTEIN, H. and WOODHOUSE, G. (1996) 'The statistical analysis of institution-based data', Ch. 10 in GOLDSTEIN, H. and LEWIS, T. (eds), *Assessment: Problems, Developments and Statistical Issues*, Chichester: John Wiley.

GRAY, J. (1996) 'The use of assessments to compare institutions', Ch. 9 in GOLDSTEIN, H. and LEWIS, T. (eds), *Assessment: Problems, Developments and Statistical Issues*, Chichester: John Wiley.

HARRIS, S., KEYS, W. and FERNANDES, C. (1997) *Third International Mathematics and Science Study (TIMSS): Second National Report*, Slough: NFER.

MANGAN, M. (1997) 'Using pupil data for primary school improvement', *Managing Schools Today*, **6**, (7).

NATIONAL COMMISSION on EDUCATION (1993) *Learning to Succeed. A Radical Look at Education Today and a Strategy for the Future*, London: Heinemann.

McPHERSON, A. (1993) 'Measuring added value in schools', Briefing Paper No. 1 for the National Commission on Education, London: Heinemann.

PFISTER, J. (1997) 'Evidence of value', *Managing Schools Today*, **6**, (8).

REYNOLDS, D. and FARRELL, S. (1996) *Worlds Apart? A Review of International Surveys of Educational Achievement Involving England*, London: HMSO.

SCAA and CSCS (May 1996) 'Using assessment results: A broadsheet for school governors', London: School Curriculum and Assessment Authority.

SHEPHARD, G. (1994) 'Value-added performance indicators for schools: A report by the school curriculum and assessment authority to the secretary of state for education, London: SCAA.

SOCIETY OF EDUCATION OFFICERS VALUE ADDED WORKING PARTY (1996) *Value Added and School Improvement*, Slough: Educational Management Information Exchange.

STRAND, S. (1998) 'A "value added" analysis of the 1996 school performance tables', *Educational Research*, **40**, (2), Summer, pp. 123–37.

WOLFENDALE, S. (1993) 'Baseline assessment: A review of current practice, issues and strategies for effective implementation', An OMEP (UK) Report, Stoke-on-Trent: Trentham Books.

Index